grow in WYCHAVON

50 business success stories of *today*...to inspire entrepreneurs and leaders of *tomorrow*

WYCHAVON DISTRICT COUNCIL
good services, good value

grow in WYCHAVON

First paperback edition printed 2013 in the United Kingdom.

A catalogue record for this book is available from the British Library.

ISBN 978-0-9508099-2-2

£9.95

Published by Wychavon District Council
To purchase more copies of this book please email communications@wychavon.gov.uk or 01386 565102

Designed and written by Wychavon District Council
www.wychavon.gov.uk

Printed in Great Britain

What people say...

"An inspirational read. A great mix of stories showing the personal face of businesses in Wychavon, and what has made them successful."

Mike Ashton
Chief Executive of Herefordshire and Worcestershire Chamber of Commerce

"This book will be a fantastic read for anyone thinking of starting their own business. Fostering new business talent is essential for the area and we're so pleased that Wychavon has pulled these stories together to inspire people."

Angela Fitch
Development Manager for Worcestershire Federation of Small Businesses

"Worcestershire Local Enterprise Partnership's aim is to create the right economic environment in the county, to inspire business, encourage investment and create lasting and sustainable employment. Publications such as 'Grow in Wychavon' provide practical tips and tools to help businesses become more successful. As such, we are happy to endorse it wholeheartedly."

Peter Pawsey
Executive Chair of Worcestershire Local Enterprise Partnership

Contents

Foreword
By Cecil Duckworth CBE

It's a real pleasure to be asked to write a foreword for Grow in Wychavon. A pleasure because this book is about two areas I'm passionate about - business and Wychavon.

Worcestershire is my adopted county. I first came here from Cheshire in 1958, to take up an apprenticeship with a local engineering company. In 1961, I qualified as a mechanical engineer and a year later, like many of the people in this book, the urge to "go it alone" became overwhelming and so in 1962, I set up my company, Worcester Engineering.

Thirty years later I sold my company to the Bosch Group and I'm proud that Worcester Bosch is still a market leader in domestic heating and hot water systems. More than that though, I'm proud that the company is still based in Worcestershire and employs nearly 2,000 people.

Since my retirement from the world of business, I have continued to back Worcestershire through a variety of ventures, from my work with Worcester Warriors Rugby Club to the various charities I support. Not least my own charity, The Duckworth Worcestershire Trust.

I am indebted to the people of Worcestershire who have supported me over the years. If, by endorsing this book, I am able to shine the spotlight on the businesses of Wychavon and encourage others to set up their own, I will be very content. I would be very happy to give advice. Wychavon District Council have been very helpful to me in business, they could not have been more co-operative.

There are many businesses and people in this book that I hadn't come across personally and I've enjoyed reading their stories, just as much as I've enjoyed reading the stories of the businesses and people I do know. The passion they all have is clear to see. These are stories to inspire, motivate and enjoy – well done Wychavon!

Cecil Duckworth CBE
Executive Chairman
Worcester Warriors

Why grow in Wychavon?
A message from the Leader and Managing Director

So why grow in Wychavon? Because it's a great place to do business. But don't take our word for it. What better way to promote the area than through the thriving businesses already here?

We wrote to businesses in Wychavon about being featured in this book, and we couldn't believe the enthusiastic response. Businesses were quick to get in touch and tell us what made them special and worthy of inclusion.

The amazing stories in this book show the diversity of businesses in Wychavon, the personal stories of the businesses and the people behind them. We hope this book will inspire others to start up, relocate or expand here.

Where is Wychavon?

Wychavon is in the heart of Worcestershire. It includes the three towns of Droitwich Spa, Evesham and Pershore, as well as nearly 100 villages and hamlets, the most well known being Broadway, often referred to as the 'Jewel of the Cotswolds'.

People love living here, and this book is all about doing business here.

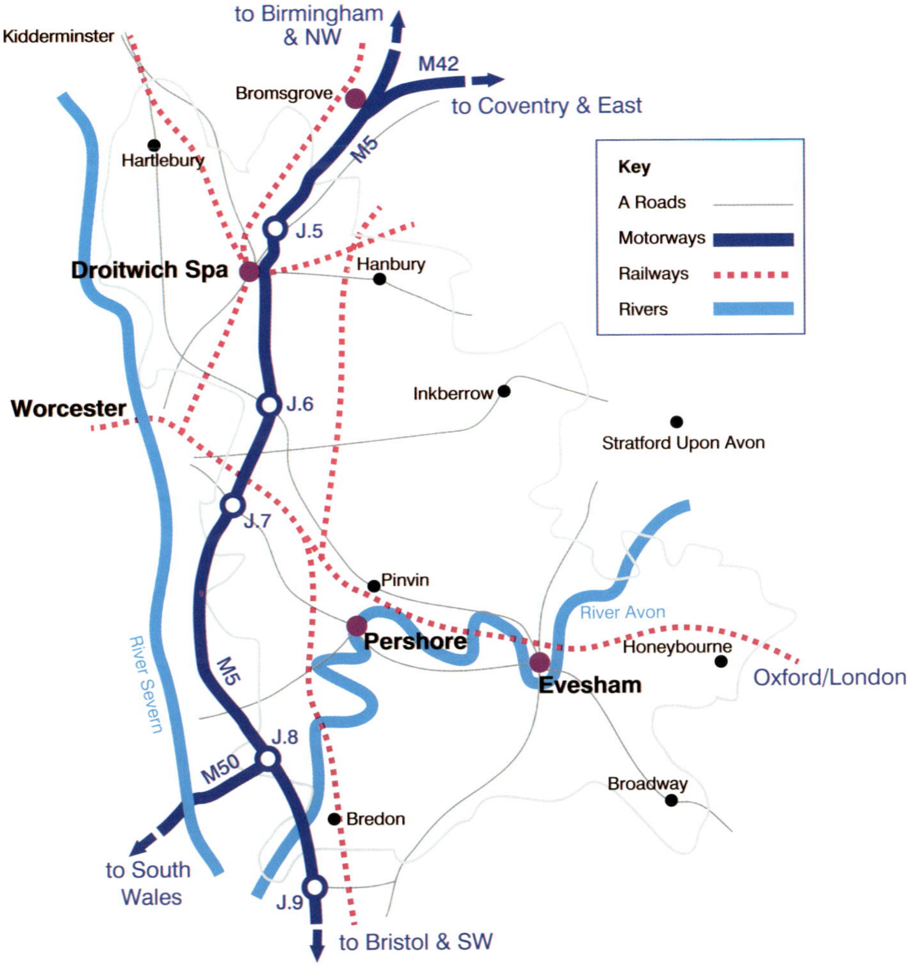
to Birmingham & NW
Kidderminster
M42
Bromsgrove
to Coventry & East
M5
Hartlebury
Key
A Roads
Motorways
Railways
Rivers
J.5
Droitwich Spa
Hanbury
Worcester
J.6
Inkberrow
Stratford Upon Avon
J.7
Pinvin
River Avon
Pershore
Honeybourne
Evesham
Oxford/London
River Severn
M5
J.8
M50
Broadway
Bredon
to South Wales
J.9
to Bristol & SW

What's in the book?

Grow in Wychavon contains the stories of 50 businesses (plus two - it was hard to decide!) reflecting different sizes and sectors from one woman bands to huge vegetable processors employing thousands. There's a chocolate maker, a breakdown truck supplier, a hotel manager, a salad grower and a Japanese knotweed eradicator. What they all have in common is that they all started or relocated their business to Wychavon. And they all have a great story to tell.

You'll read about the issues these business people faced and how they overcame them, the decisions they had to make and their business lessons to share. You'll read why they picked Wychavon as the place for their business and how the lifestyle and location work together to provide a great offering.

Whether or not you live or work in Wychavon, if you're interested in business and business people, and what motivates them, then this book will fascinate you. We hope it might just inspire you to think about setting up your own business here too.

And finally...

We'd like to thank all the businesses that got involved. We couldn't feature everyone, but we appreciate the time people took to get in touch with us and share their stories, even if they aren't included in the book.

We'd also like to thank the Design Council for their input into this project that has led to this innovation. I am really pleased with the Design Council's challenge, which has made us focus more on attracting, up-skilling and growing to aid economic development.

Particular thanks to Fiona Narburgh and Emma Wild for interviewing, compiling and editing the stories, Helen Keegan for designing the book, Mo Cook for co-ordinating the feedback and to our partners, Blue Chilli Marketing Ltd and JDA Media for working with us on this exciting project.

For more information, including interviews with the businesses featured and information on those that aren't included in the book, go to **www.growinwychavon.co.uk**

Councillor Paul Middlebrough
Leader of Wychavon District Council

Jack Hegarty
Managing Director of Wychavon District Council

Why Wychavon?
A message from the editors

We've really enjoyed interviewing the people in this book, finding out what makes their businesses special, what advice they'd offer people starting out in their careers and what motivates them to get out of bed every morning (as well as the alarm clock!)

We especially wanted to find out what businesses love about being based here and the benefits the area has to offer. We didn't expect people to be quite as enthusiastic about our location as they were. We certainly found some very passionate advocates for the district.

There are **five Cs** that we consistently heard as people shared their stories with us about why the location is important to them. They are:

1. Central – right in the middle of England.
2. Countryside – people just love it here, our gorgeous green and fertile land.
3. Culture – parks, cinemas, theatres, big cities – all on our doorstep.
4. Competent workforce – enthusiastic, skilled people.
5. Council – helpful and supportive with grants and advice.

So here's a selection of quotes from what people told us...

"We're on the way to everywhere."
Penelope Bossom, Overbury Estate

"A lot of our competitors are based in London and Birmingham but we've got such excellent transport links around here that it doesn't matter."
Nick Gray, GTech

"We can get an order in the morning from someone up in Scotland and the goods can be with them by the evening. There's also a great community spirit here..."
Andrew Bille, Evesham Vale Growers

"It really was a lifestyle choice to settle here. Pershore is a safe and secure place and my children are very happy at the local school."
Clive Brooker, Environet UK Ltd

"We're in an area that is great for growing. I've always considered the Vale of Evesham to be the undiscovered 'garden of England'..."
Judy Gardner, Eckington Manor

"It's a wonderful location to do business, there are great links, clients love that it's peaceful and quiet."
Dale Parmenter, DRP Group

"A beautiful view definitely gets the creative juices flowing...and when you're the Managing Director of a product design company that creativity is vital."
Derrick Barker, JMDA

"I love being based in Droitwich Spa...we're on the edge of the industrial heartland of England..and close to Birmingham Airport."
Phil Marsay-Jones, Cepha Controls

"We chose Pershore because it has everything to hand, it's compact, well-connected and we can reach our London-based clients in just two hours by train. Our team love where we are as well. They're always using the leisure centre for a good workout..."
Victoria Poole, Poole Phillips Associates

"I love the Cotswolds and the Evesham area; I love the river, the Malvern Hills, the architecture and the parks. Evesham has a lovely feel to it and I just fell in love with the town."

Kim Beckley, Kim Jewellery Ltd

"There are some excellent hotels with very high-quality restaurants and nobody can be more passionate about selling an area than someone who lives here."

Viv Hudson, Hotelshop UK Ltd

"We've got some fantastic apprentices with us and it's great to see them developing and being promoted…our co-director was 17 when he started here, sweeping the floor. Now he owns 20 percent of the company. That's the kind of person we're looking for, and we're confident that we're in the best place to find them."

Rod Smith, Winstanley

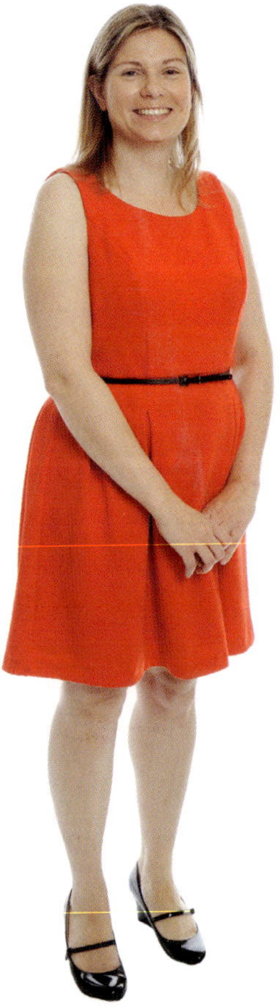

"Being based in the Wychavon district meant we were able to secure some funding and soft loans from the Council at the beginning of the project. They've been very supportive."

Laurence Wiper, The Regal Cinema

"The council has really supported me as a business. They let me pay my business rates over 12 months instead of ten, which helped a lot with cash flow. They also gave me a £1,000 grant when we moved into our premises in Pershore Business Park to help us update our IT equipment."

Steve Cooper, S E Cooper Iron Works

"I've always worked well with Wychavon's environmental health officers who I know can help me to get to where I need to be, which will help me grow my business."
Kit Bamford, Kit's Kitchen

We hope you enjoy reading Grow in Wychavon as much as we've enjoyed researching and editing the stories.

Fiona Narburgh (Pictured right)
Head of Strategy and Communications
Wychavon District Council

Emma Wild (Pictured left)
Communications Manager
Wychavon District Council

P.S. Delve in where you like – the businesses aren't in any particular order!

1.

Nick Grey

Gtech

A design company specialising in cordless floor-care products

Business start date
2001

Number of employees
57

Location
Spetchley

www.gtechonline.co.uk

Nick's business lesson

"Be careful with your cash. Everyone wants you to spend money; suppliers, service providers and bank managers. You have very limited resources so be diligent with what you have."

Nick Grey is a man on a mission...he wants to design the best-loved floor-care products that have ever been made, and he's doing it right here in Spetchley, in Wychavon.

The road to Nick's success is an interesting one. It was 2001 when he resigned from his position as Head of Product Development at a vacuum manufacturer and decided to go it alone. Armed with a passion for design and enough savings to last him 18 months, he had a strict plan. Nick explains, "I knew I didn't want to get into debt so I set myself a time frame to stick to. It's easy to spend money but it's much harder to make it, so I was realistic with myself. At the end of those 18 months I was either going to have developed a product that I could sell and turn into a viable business, or I was going to have to go and get a job. Luckily, I developed a great product and Gtech was born in 2002."

It took a lot of hard work and dedication before Nick was happy with his first product, which was a cordless floor sweeper. "I'd go round to my mum's house every week and we'd try it out. She had two big black Labradors and trying to get the hair out of the carpet was a nightmare. It took a long time but we got there eventually," Nick comments. "I remember sitting one night thinking that I could sell 10 million of those sweepers. It was a great product and it was better than anything else on the market. We've now sold over 20 million of them."

Nick's ethos is simple, "I'm my own biggest critic and I'm a very particular customer. At Gtech we strive to design products that have at least one advantage over the competition. It's important to design the product from the consumer's perspective. Will they be able to get better elsewhere? If the answer is yes, it's time to go back to the drawing board. You need to make sure that 99 percent of the product is as good as your competitors. The other one percent has to be even better."

Born and raised in Bromsgrove, Nick didn't even consider taking his business anywhere else when he first set up and he hasn't got any plans to move in the future. "I've always been here. I have to go to London and New York sometimes, but there's nowhere else that I need to be based other than right here," he comments. "Ever since I've been in business I've had cows sitting in a field next to me and I couldn't imagine not working with them looking at me; it feels right for me to be in a rural area. A lot of our competitors are based in London and Birmingham, but we've got such excellent transport links around here that it doesn't matter."

For Nick, it's the support of the people around him that has helped him get to where he is now. He's a strong advocate for surrounding himself with trusted advisors. He explains, "As soon as it's warranted, I'd really recommend having a good management team and colleagues around you. They can be the difference between success and failure. My team have really helped me out, they act as someone you can bounce ideas off, which is how ideas and products are developed."

Gtech has also scooped awards, 'Business of the Year' and 'Excellence in Innovation' at the 2013 Herefordshire and Worcestershire Chamber of Commerce awards.

2.

Lucy Howson

Vanilla Moon

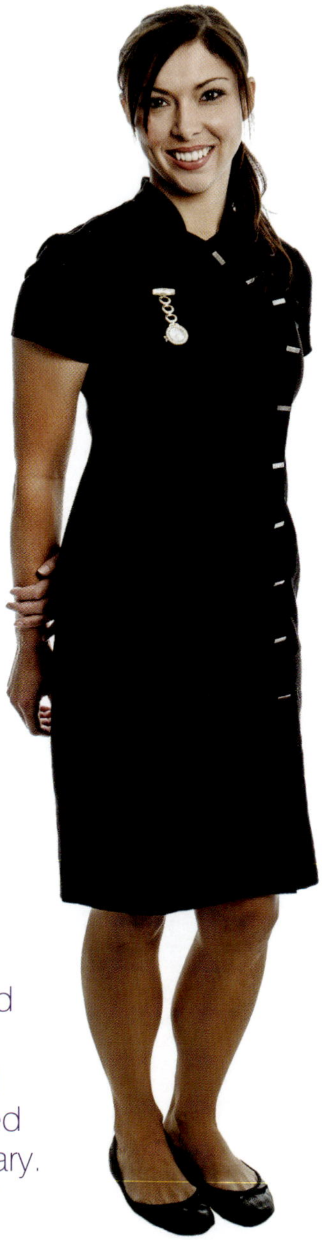

Organic and holistic beauty in tranquil surroundings, with treatments suited to each person's individual needs

Business start date
2012

Number of employees
1

Location
Bridge Street, Evesham

www.vanillamooncotswolds.co.uk

Lucy's business lesson

"If you really want to achieve something, you need to be prepared to make sacrifices. I had to make some big cut backs in order to fund myself through college but I just used to tell myself that it was only temporary. Keep thinking of the bigger picture."

If you're looking for a calming massage look no further than Vanilla Moon in Evesham. You'll get a pretty inspiring story from owner Lucy Howson too.

If anyone had told Lucy Howson three years ago that she'd be running her own successful holistic and beauty salon she would have laughed and said "no chance." After being made redundant from her previous job working in export, Lucy was desperate, but it turned out to be a blessing in disguise. "I'm a strong believer that everything happens for a reason and being made redundant gave me the chance to re-train in something I was passionate about," she explains.

Making the decision to go back to college was tough, "I'm a single mum and was told that being in full-time education and looking after my son wouldn't work, and I wouldn't receive any financial help," Lucy says. "It was a difficult decision but I just decided to go for it. South Worcestershire College was great and the support I received was fantastic."

Lucy was named Student of the Year in 2011 and was put forward to compete in an international skills competition along with two other students, where they finished in the top six. "I wasn't very good at school but I loved being at college. I'd found something I was really interested in and I was really focused and committed. I made some big sacrifices and really had to cut back but it was worth it when Vanilla Moon opened last year. The icing on the cake was being awarded the Small Business Entrepreneur 2012 by the Chamber of Commerce. It was a huge achievement and I'm really proud of how far I've come," she comments.

As an Evesham girl through and through, Lucy didn't even consider opening her salon anywhere else. She was awarded a start-up grant by Wychavon District Council, which allowed her to purchase the basic equipment she needed to open up the business. Located at the bottom of Bridge Street, Vanilla Moon sits in a pretty courtyard that suits the relaxed nature of the salon perfectly. Lucy enthuses, "Evesham is a great little place to have a business. Most of my clients hear about me through word of mouth and they're all very loyal. There are only a few other salons in the area and we all get on really well, which means there's no nasty competitiveness and we all support one another."

Lucy is one of South Worcestershire College's success stories. Not only is she in talks with the college to become a part-time lecturer, but she was also invited back as a guest speaker at the annual college award ceremony.

3.

Judy Gardner

Eckington Manor

Luxury bed and breakfast, cookery school, restaurant and farm

Business start date
2007

Number of employees
23

Location
Eckington

www.eckingtonmanor.co.uk

Judy's business lesson

"Have integrity in everything you do, and never compromise on quality."

You know straight away when you meet Judy Gardner that you're in the company of someone who puts high-quality produce at the centre of everything she does. She has an inspirational story to tell; one that starts with a small fruit and veg shop and ends with a 300-acre empire!

When Judy moved to Pershore following her divorce, she didn't know anyone. But all that changed when she opened up her small fruit and veg shop. She comments, "I had no experience in fresh produce but the outlay was quite small. I'm quite business-minded so decided to give it a go. It was a blessing really, because getting out and selling the produce in the local community meant I got to know people. Plus, because it was fresh it gave me extra incentive to be chatty with my customers and work hard to shift it!"

With business booming, Judy decided to expand her range with the introduction of her own range of pickles and chutneys. She says, "I started selling them in the shop and one of my customers decided to send a few jars to Sainsbury's, Waitrose and Fortnum & Mason. I didn't expect much to come of it, but Fortnum & Mason put in an order and before I knew it, Garner's pickles were being sold in all the large supermarket chains. It was an exciting time for me."

It wasn't long before Baxters took an interest in Garner's pickles, and in 2001, she sold the business. It gave Judy the opportunity and funds to take her love of food and local produce in a new direction. It was in 2005 when she bought the run down Eckington Manor farm and the rest, as they say, is history.

"Food, and particularly the quality of food, has always been very important to me and I'm proud to be able to say that food is very much at the heart of my business today," Judy explains. "At Eckington Manor we grow our own vegetables and rear our own beef and lamb, sharing them with our customers through our cookery school and restaurant. We also converted some of

the historic farm buildings here to provide luxury five star accommodation allowing our guests to enjoy a relaxing stay in peaceful surroundings." And that's where a place like Eckington, near Pershore, really comes into its own. Judy adds, "We're in an area that is great for growing. I've always considered the Vale of Evesham to be the undiscovered 'garden of England', and the rural landscape is stunning to wake up to."

From day one in the fruit and veg shop, Judy's approach has always been one of integrity, quality, honesty and perseverance. "I'd never knowingly sell a squidgy tomato; I started out with strong principles and I've stayed true to them right the way through," she comments. "I believe that by maintaining complete control of my family run business, I've been able to ensure that quality is never compromised. Even when times were tough, I resisted the temptation to sell equity and am thankful for not doing so."

Judy places a strong emphasis on supporting the local area and its people. She comments, "I feel it's important to share success where possible and in doing so, help grow the local economy by employing local people, purchasing from local food producers and through investing in property. I own property in Eckington and Pershore that I rent out, providing premises for local businesses, as well as homes. I like to think that has kept some of my success within Wychavon."

As well as sharing success, Judy shares her love of food through her cookery school. "It's lovely meeting people and finding out why they wanted to come to the school. Some have received vouchers as gifts and others want to develop their existing skills. We had a lovely 90 year old gentleman, happily married for 60 years, whose wife had recently passed away. In his words 'she'd only ever cooked chicken!' and he was keen to add a bit of variety to his diet. He went away having had a lovely time, with a repertoire of new beef and lamb recipes...and a big smile on his face."

4.

Bal Padda

Vicarage Nurseries

Award-winning soft fruit growers

Business start date
1996

Number of employees
10 permanent
300+ seasonal workers

Location
Bretforton

www.vicaragenurseries.co.uk

Bal's business lesson

"Set a goal and then surround yourself with people who believe you can achieve it."

Vicarage Nurseries began as a one-man operation when Makhan Singh Padda bought the land in 1996. What started out as an interesting hobby is now an award-winning business producing strawberries for a leading supermarket chain.

If there's a perfect example of believing in your own ability to succeed, Vicarage Nurseries is it. Business owner Makhan Singh Padda came to the UK in 1966 from the Punjab, India, determined to work hard to support his family. After taking on a variety of jobs he turned his hand to packing strawberries, and that was when a colleague asked why he wasn't using his existing farming skills to produce strawberries, rather than just pack them. This idea came to fruition when Makhan bought Vicarage Nurseries in 1996. Back then it covered just 2.6 acres. Now it spans over 200.

Continuing to work to support his family, Makhan spent his spare time growing different strawberry varieties to see which gave the best yield and before long, he became an established grower supplying to markets. In that time, Makhan was joined by Jas Singh, his first full-time employee. Jas had come to the UK in 1996 and gained experience in warehouse management. While working with Makhan, he furthered his knowledge of the technical side of growing and became a self-taught agronomist.

In 2009, Makhan's son Bal Padda joined the family business, bringing with him 15 years' packhouse experience. Vicarage Nurseries still had a very small team in place when an approach came from Asda's buying arm, International Produce Limited (IPL), in September 2009. Through IPL, Asda was looking for a UK grower to serve them directly and they were keen to work closely with Vicarage Nurseries to develop a relationship.

Bal explains, "My Dad had only ever supplied into markets and from my experience as production manager in a packhouse environment, I knew that retailers had very stringent requirements. We were nervous and a bit dubious, but very excited at the same time."

After much consideration and a lot of encouragement and support from IPL, Vicarage Nurseries put in its proposal and the relationship commenced. "Building up the team to cope with the demands was the first thing to do," says Bal. "People within the industry were telling us that we needed to bring in retail experts to succeed, but we had other ideas. We were determined to learn 'on the job'. My dad, Jas and I decided that Vicarage Nurseries would be all about quality, and to deliver that quality we'd need quality people. We already had some excellent people working as pickers and supervisors so we built our quality-driven team from the ground up." Bal continues, "We set ourselves a goal and surrounded ourselves with people who believed we could achieve it."

There was positivity in abundance and a real determination to make it work, but the weather wasn't so supportive. "In our first year establishing ourselves as professional growers, we had to endure the worst winter for 30 years, referred to in the media as 'the big freeze', followed by some really wet summers. We certainly didn't have an easy time of it!"

But strawberries have long been associated with love and for Vicarage Nurseries, this romantic story does have a happy ending, and a rosy future.

"Our focus on quality worked," says Bal. "Even in the wettest summers, our quality scores were exceptional. We did receive valuable advice from local growers and in 2012, we received the coveted 'Soft Fruit Grower of the Year Award'.

In a professional capacity, it's still early days at Vicarage Nurseries. In 2009, the business employed just two full-time staff and 40 seasonal workers. By 2013, those numbers had increased dramatically to ten full-time staff and over 300 seasonal workers. "Our staff are everything," concludes Bal. "We believed in them and they believed in us...we're achieving this together."

5.

David Chill

Mr Chill's Traditional Sweet Emporium and Versatility in Print

Traditional sweet shop, printing and graphic design

Business start date
2003

Number of employees
14

Location
Mr Chill's Sweets - Evesham/Birmingham

Versatility in Printing and Ribbon Printing Co Europe - Droitwich Spa

www.traditional-sweets.co.uk
www.vipprinters.co.uk
www.ribbonprintingeurope.com

David's business lesson

"I like to inject a bit of fun into everything I try, and I always try everything at least once."

David Chill has a passion for all things traditional and it's in his printing business and nostalgic sweet shop where this love of old-fashioned ways really comes to life.

It took 23 years and a number of successful stints in hotel management positions before David Chill realised where he really wanted his future to lie. Straight out of college, David went into the hotel trade and worked his way up from kitchen porter to junior manager, and then to deputy general manager of the former Pine Lodge Hotel in Bromsgrove, achieving four star status and two AA Rosettes. For the last three years of his hotel career, David ran the Fownes Hotel in Worcester.

It was at this point that a printing works caught his eye. David explains, "I'd always had an interest in printing processes, particular those using Hot Foil to achieve a high-quality gold or silver finish. An opportunity was there to buy out a local printing press from a retiring owner and I was keen, but needed to raise the funds."

And that's where sweets came into play!

"To raise the money needed, I ventured out into traditional sweets and took a stall at the Worcester Victorian Christmas Fayre," David explains. "The sweets went down a storm. The customers loved the nostalgic selection so I took every opportunity to sell them at markets until I raised enough to add to my life savings and buy the Hot Foil press business."

David began developing the printing business under the name Versatility in Print. Alongside this business he also offers specialist ribbon printing and the luxury Hot Foils press. Three years later in 2007, David was asked if he'd be interested in taking over the running of the sweet shop at the National Trust Back to Backs Houses in Birmingham, which he did.

Nougat Almond
Rock
Edinburgh Rock
Sugared Almonds
Floral Gums
Cherry Lips Scented
Lion's Sports Mixture
Lion's Poor Bens
Lion's Midget Gems
Bon Bons Chocolate
Dandelion and Burdock
Cola Cubes
Pineapple Chunks
Blackberry and Apple
Rosy Apples
Blackberries and Raspberries
Sweet Peanuts
SWEETS BY THE QUARTER
BUBBLEGUM PIPS
RASPBERRY PIPS
APPLE PIPS
Pips Sherbet
Sherbets Lemon
Sherbets Strawberry
Fruit Pastilles
Fruit Jellies
Sweet Tobacco
Plum and Custard

Slowly but surely this business grew. "Customers' reactions to these old-fashioned sweets, sold by the quarter or the half pound, were so positive, and our focus on delivering attentively was also really appreciated," David explains. "This gave us the confidence to start looking for premises to open our second 'Mr Chill's Sweet Emporium'. We trawled Worcestershire, viewing seven or eight really good options, before settling on our shop at the bottom of Bridge Street in Evesham – a great location for passing custom." This was closely followed by a third shop in 2011 at Evesham Country Park, which is run by David's wife.

Sarsaparilla tablets, winter mix, aniseed twists, cinnamon balls...they're all there at Mr Chill's, along with David's favourite lemon bon bons, which he says aren't kind to his fillings! It's the production process that makes David's sweets extra special. "Our hard boiled sweets are made by artisan producers in Britain, many are in the West Midlands." He explains, "They're hand boiled in 42 kilogram batches in old-fashioned copper pots before the mixture is poured onto cold steel slabs before being hand rolled, flavoured and made into sweets. For sweet-lovers out there, it's fantastic to watch, and the sweets are fantastic to eat!"

David's most recent venture has been to create a sweet based on a fruit that is synonymous with the area – the black pear. David's Worcestershire Black Pear sweet was officially launched in 2013 and is a lovely local sweet for the area.

6.

Polly Gowers

Everyclick

Online fundraising tool
for UK charities

Business start date
2007

Number of employees
20

Location
Vale Business Park, Evesham

www.giveasyoulive.com

Polly's business lesson

"Never, ever give up!"

Philanthropic is just one way to describe Everyclick CEO and founder Polly Gowers. But the enthusiastic entrepreneur, who was recently named as one of the most influential women in IT by ComputerWeekly, started her business in her garden shed.

Back in 2005, Polly Gowers was running a small marketing agency when she got the idea for Everyclick. "I was talking to a colleague about her fundraising efforts for Save the Children," she explains. "She happened to mention how great it would be if she could raise money using search engines. It was a brilliant idea. Traditionally each time a search engine is used a small amount of money is paid to the company behind the search engine. But there's no reason why this money couldn't go to charity instead." With that, Everyclick was born.

Polly set to work writing up a business plan and raising the capital needed to fund the IT platform. She transformed her garden shed into an office and now, seven years on, she's raised over £4 million for UK charities, has a team of 19 and a large and spacious office in Evesham.

Everyclick is set up as a social enterprise and is structured so that 50 percent of all of the money generated goes to charity. The remaining 50 percent is reinvested back into the business to pay employees and develop the IT platform to allow the business to grow.

Since its humble back-garden beginnings, Everyclick has grown phenomenally and now includes a piece of sister software called Give as you Live. Polly comments, "In terms of search engines, we're never going to be as big as Google, which is fine! We just focus our efforts on growing in other ways, which is how 'Give as you Live' developed."

Working in a similar way to the Everyclick platform, Give as you Live offers users the chance to donate money when they shop online. What's more, it doesn't cost the user a penny. "We've developed relationships with thousands of big brands, such as Selfridges, Tesco and Smythson, who have all agreed to donate a commission on every online purchase to charity. Traditionally, that commission would have been paid to the search engine that recommended them to the shopper in the first place," Polly says. "The best part is that it doesn't cost the consumer anything. We've had shoppers who, in less than 12 months, have raised over £1,000 for charity, just by buying what they already buy online. All they have to do is either install our shopping bar on their computer tool bar, or visit the Give as you Live website and click on our link to visit the retailer's website."

To date, Polly has over 140 investors but finding funding for her venture wasn't easy. "It took a lot to convince people that it was worthwhile. It was quite tough to get the charities involved as well, but as we've grown more and more are coming on board." She explains, "We currently raise money for about 220,000 charities, and when our users sign up they're able to pick which one to donate to."

As far as the IT industry is concerned, Polly is a force to be reckoned with. She was named as one of the most influential women in IT by ComputerWeekly, Give as you Live was voted as 'The Most Promising UK Internet Company' and it won the 'People's Choice Award' at the Internet World Awards 2013.

Oh, and did we mention that she was awarded an OBE in 2012 for her services to philanthropy in the UK? Polly says, "Receiving my OBE has spurred me on even more. The beauty of Give as you Live and Everyclick is that it enables everyone to be a philanthropist, every day."

7.

Clive Champion and Roger Beard

Kanes Foods Ltd

Processors of fresh, chilled vegetables as 'ready to eat packs' for major UK supermarkets

Business start date
1989

Number of employees
1,800

Location
Middle Littleton

www.kanesfoods.co.uk

Roger and Clive's business lesson

"Always be fair to your staff, suppliers and customers. Add value to your product and your brand wherever possible, this becomes your reputation."

When the founder of Kanes Foods, John Randall, died in July 2011, it became the responsibility of Roger Beard and Clive Champion, alongside two other directors, to run the pre-packed salad business. Even though John is no longer with them, his ethos is still strong.

As the largest private sector employer in the district with 1,800 employees, Kanes Foods has a big impact on the local area's economy, not only as an employer but also as a direct customer to many of the local growers. Kanes Foods processes and supplies fresh, chilled vegetables as 'ready to eat packs' for major supermarkets in the UK. Products include over 20 different types of salad bags, layered salad trays, deli components, bean sprouts, stir fry vegetables and fresh noodles. Every week, the company processes over 300 tonnes of salad from its four factories on the 28-acre site in Middle Littleton, near Evesham.

If any of your journeys around Wychavon have taken you past the Kanes Foods building, you'll know about it. Especially if that journey happened after July 2012 when Kanes' innovative salad processing unit officially opened with its state-of-the-art biodiverse wild flower grass roof.

Clive Champion, Projects and Engineering Director, picks up the story. "We needed to grow our capacity for bagged salad processing and with that, we needed to ensure that we had a highly technical operation with consistent output. Our founder, John Randall, was always very focused on innovation and happy to invest if it gave the company a unique edge to support our 'proud to be different' motto."

As well as the need to introduce a highly advanced processing facility that would offer a modern and very comfortable working environment, it was equally important for the company to ensure that this new £30 million facility was sympathetic to its rural surroundings. It needed to blend in with the environment, not jar it. The meadow roof, which is planted with nearly 90 wild flower species and is thought to be the largest of its kind in the UK, was officially opened by TV presenter and botanist James Wong.

Innovation is certainly a company watchword and the new salad processing unit is a clear example of this in practice. Fairness is another philosophy advocated by John Randall and fully supported by Kanes Foods' four directors today. "Having worked with John at Kanes for 12 years, I know how much importance he placed on always being fair - fair to employees, fair to suppliers and fair to customers," explains Roger Beard, Finance Director. "He firmly believed that this fairness would be reciprocated and the company would be successful as a result. We rely on our suppliers to provide us with high-quality produce and we've developed very positive long-standing relationships with many of the growers in the Vale. We work together to innovate and to make sure that, collectively, we're able to produce and supply what the end customer needs."

Continuing with the company founder's ethos of fairness, Kanes Foods employs its staff directly and invests heavily in its own staff recruitment and training, rather than using gangmaster labour agencies. "Over the past seven years, we've seen new communities develop as Polish, Lithuanian and Latvian migrants have come to the UK to work hard and make a new future for themselves and their families," Roger comments.

The food industry is one that doesn't stand still, there are always new salad varieties and added value packaging options to put forward to customers. And do Roger and Clive have a personal favourite, maybe one of the new types of salad leaf? "It's a traditional iceberg for me, I like the crunch," says Roger. And for Clive? "I like something with a bit more flavour, I'm more of a peppery kind of man," he comments. But as with any industry where you're surrounded by the produce day in, day out, you probably opt for something else entirely when given the choice!

8.

Julie Howson

Smart Exchange

Dress and bridal agency

Business start date
2006

Number of employees
2

Location
High Street, Pershore

www.smartexchange-pershore.co.uk

Julie's business lesson

"Take advantage of the help and advice that's available to you. Visit your bank, speak to your local council and see what learning providers can do for you."

Sitting pretty in a prime position on Pershore's High Street is a little gem that's well known amongst the women of Wychavon. From designer weekend wear to prom dresses and bridal gowns, Julie Howson stocks it all.

"My husband thought I was mad when I told him I was going to quit my job to open up my own dress agency," laughs Julie Howson, owner of Smart Exchange in Pershore. "I used to work as a designer for a global packaging company in Surrey but it got to the point where I'd had enough of the business world. I wasn't achieving a very good work/life balance so I just decided to take the plunge and open up my own designer dress agency."

The concept behind Smart Exchange is simple. The shop is packed full of beautiful second hand designer pieces that are on sale for around 50 percent less than the original retail price. It's not a vintage shop, although designer vintage handbags sell well, and all the pieces for sale are sold as new and are less than two years old. It's become the go-to place for discerning ladies looking for something special because of the high-quality, fashionable items available. The pre-loved items are inspected fully to make sure they're in a great condition and a lot of the items for sale even have the original labels on them. Julie explains, "Our ladies bring in those clothes that might have been bought for a special occasion and have only been worn once, or have been languishing unloved at the back of the wardrobe. We then sell them on their behalf."

Julie regularly gets customers coming to her that have been recommended by businesses in the area. She says, "We recently kitted out a French lady who was staying at a hotel in Broadway. Her luggage had been lost on her way over here for her daughter's wedding and the hotel put her in a taxi and sent her our way, which was really nice."

Recently, Julie has noticed a big change in the wedding industry. More and more brides are coming into the shop to check out what's on offer and she's happily taken on the role of fairy godmother. She enthuses, "We recently had a bride come in who'd bought a wedding dress online. She was really disappointed with it when it arrived but didn't think she'd be able to find anything else. She came in to us on a whim and needless to say, we sent her away with a beautiful new gown. We get to work with some really lovely people, at really important times of their lives. It's great."

Since Smart Exchange opened in 2006, Julie has witnessed a shift in her customer base. She says, "People's attitude towards shopping is changing. It's helped that the Duchess of Cambridge is quite a famous fan of dress agencies too, as a lot of people think that if it's good enough for a Royal then it's good enough for them."

9.

Ken and Paul Felton

Fruit Salad

Greengrocers

Business start date
1988

Number of employees
5

Location
High Street, Pershore

Ken's business lesson

"It's quality and service every time for me, customers remember those long after price."

Fruit and veg fresh from the grower and some good old-fashioned customer service with time for a chat, are what work for father and son team Ken and Paul Felton.

For anyone who wants to buy the freshest fruit and veg possible, then it has to be from Fruit Salad – Pershore's long-standing, High Street greengrocer. Ken Felton has been running Fruit Salad for 25 years after setting it up in September 1988, and his son Paul joined him ten years later to complete the partnership.

Ken explains, "We didn't really set out to be a father and son team. I asked Paul to 'give me a hand' over a busy Christmas period when he was in between jobs, and he never left! Fifteen years on and he knows many of the customers by their first name and we have a brilliant working relationship."

Being based in the heart of the Vale of Evesham, Fruit Salad has access to an abundance of high-quality fruit and veg from a number of local growers – harvested one day, sold to customers the next. Or even the very same day! Paul explains,"When it's strawberry season they're picked early in the morning, collected from the grower by Dad or me and in our shop by 9am for customers to enjoy. It's like that with all our produce, straight from the grower and into our shop – no need for markets or wholesalers."

Pershore is a relaxed place surrounded by greenery and orchards, but the High Street itself has quite a buzz, much of which Ken attributes to the fact that, for people who live there, shopping is a social event. "You can pop in and out of a supermarket and not speak to anyone at all, but when people come into our shop, we want to know how they are and hear their stories.

"We heard a story recently from a customer who had friends to stay from London. She asked her husband to pop out for half a dozen things and when he hadn't returned over two hours later, her friends were quite concerned," Ken says. "And the lady said to her visitors, 'That's Pershore for you - you go up town and meet the world and his wife so you just chat!'"

The famous Plum Festival sets Pershore's heart beating for four weeks every summer and it's a busy time for Ken and Paul too. "People travel from around the region and beyond to experience the festival. They always want to take some plums back home so when they pop in to see us, we're happy to provide them with lovely fresh produce and a very warm, friendly Pershore welcome!"

10.

Nikki Moran

Vale Balloons

Professional balloon decorating service and party supplies shop for all occasions

Business start date
2006

Number of employees
2

Location
Avon Street, Evesham

www.valeballoons.co.uk

Nikki's business lesson

"Sell yourself. Your customers need to like you and trust you, because they'll find an alternative if they don't."

Take one look at the amazing displays that Nikki and her team at Vale Balloons design and you'll know that there's a lot more to balloons than just hot air.

Nikki Moran got into the balloon business by accident. Seven years ago, she used to have a stall at Evesham market selling handbags and shoes. When the local florist left the market, she left behind a helium cylinder and a few foil balloons. The rest, as they say, is history.

Nikki explains, "My sister, who had a stall next to me, took on the balloons at first. But the extra work was too much so I offered to help out and I discovered that I loved balloons! I really enjoyed working with them, but I realised quite quickly that I needed to learn more about them, so I signed up to do a Balloon Fundamentals Course."

The course taught Nikki the basics about balloons and balloon design, including all the technical information she needed to know about helium, how to make an arch and what sort of machinery she'd need to start her own business. "It was an eye-opener," she says. "There's a massive, multi-million pound industry out there that I knew nothing about. It was really exciting. Since that one day course, I've attended lots more, including wedding and corporate decor and balloon structures. I'm always learning and signing up to new courses all the time."

She's so committed to her profession that Nikki now holds Certified Balloon Artist (CBA) status, which is the industry's top professional qualification. The CBA recognises dedicated individuals who have achieved the highest level of skill and ability in balloon decorating. Nikki laughs, "When I tell people I have this qualification it always makes them smile. But it was hard work and it helps to separate me from other people in the industry."

Renowned in the area for providing top-quality balloons, Nikki's customers come from all over. She comments, "We're based in Evesham and we get a lot of local business. But because we're centrally located, we get a lot of business from places like Stratford, Worcester and Cheltenham too. We have really good relationships with a lot of hotels in the surrounding areas, who put their guests in touch with us if they're planning a big event."

The ability of balloons to make people smile is one of the reasons Nikki loves her job. Vale Balloons provides balloon decorating for special occasions and a lot of their customers use them for important milestones. She says, "We're often involved with people's celebrations from the engagement party to the wedding. We go on to do the balloons when the children are born, when they're christened and when they celebrate their birthdays. We get to know our customers really well and they trust us."

Nikki feels a lot of responsibility towards her customers but she relishes the part she plays in their celebrations. She enthuses, "Because of the nature of the business, it's really important that we always deliver. My customers can't change the date of the wedding or push back their birthday because we're behind schedule, so we work hard to make sure we don't let anyone down. It's tough but it's so rewarding. There's something magical about balloons, and seeing people's faces light up when they see what we've created makes all the early starts and late nights worth it."

11.

Mark Pickford

Electron Commercial Utilities Ltd

Commercial energy consultants

Business start date
2007

Number of employees
4

Location
Evesham

www.electroncommercial.com

Mark's business lesson

"Focus on long term relationships."

Seeking out the very best energy deal for his business customers is what's been keeping Mark Pickford busy for the last 14 years.

As owner of Electron Commercial Utilities Ltd, alongside partner Jane Dickinson, Mark is focused on helping businesses to save on their energy bills, wherever possible. Back in 1999, Mark and Jane were both employed at Powergen (now E.ON) and getting increasingly frustrated with the red tape and do's and don'ts associated with working for a big energy supplier. It was time for a change. A new era of energy supply was on the horizon, following the industry's deregulation, and by becoming a sole agent for a number of the smaller suppliers, Electron Commercial Utilities set about its mission to help companies to save on their bills.

"From day one it was all about trust," says Mark. "We wanted people to come to us, see what we could do for them, and then make their own decisions based on the information provided. We don't ask our customers to sign a contract with us. If they like what we find for them the only contract they have is with the energy supplier, and we have relationships in place with the big six."

This approach to business has helped Mark to build a loyal customer base, which includes retailer Holland and Barrett, and many clients involved in farming and agriculture. In 2013, Electron Commercial Utilities became an affinity partner for NSF International, the most widely known and respected food assurance brand, which enables compliant producers to use the Red Tractor logo on their food. It was a big win for Mark and the team.

Mark continues, "It's more important to me to look after the customers that I have than it is to go chasing after new ones. We have very high customer retention rate."

And new options for helping customers to save on energy bills are presenting themselves all the time. In addition to acting as a broker for utility companies, Mark is often asked for recommendations in the 'green' energy sectors. "We work with close and trusted associates who have substantial experience in this sector. They've not just popped up in the last few months as many others have," comments Mark. "A current project where we've replaced all halogens with LEDs for a high street chain is set to deliver 70% savings on their energy bill. Now that's the type of customer-focused service that keeps me excited about the future."

Mark is originally from south Birmingham but Evesham is where his partner, Jane, grew up. "It was the natural choice for us to set up in Evesham. Apart from the family connections and the lovely surroundings, it's got great motorway networks - in the car I can pretty much get everywhere I need to be within two hours," says Mark.

12.

Phil Checketts

Checketts Fine Foods

A destination shop for lovers of good meat, fresh fish, fine cheeses, coffee and all you would expect of a delicatessen

Business start date
1902

Number of employees
20

Location
Ombersley

www.checketts.co.uk

Phil's business lesson

"Keep your customers happy with excellent quality and the very best of service. Also pay attention to your profit margins."

Crispy crackling, beautiful beef joints and sumptuous sausages have been available from Checketts Fine Foods for over 100 years. But most recently, owner Phil has expanded his offering to keep up with demand.

Checketts Fine Foods has a lot of history. Back in 1902, grandfather Checketts opened up his first butcher's shop in the small village of Wyre Piddle, then moved to a shop in Ombersley Road, Worcester. The little shop became famous for the top-quality meat available and the outstanding level of customer service and quickly outgrew the premises. In 1925, the shop moved to Ombersley where it's been expanding ever since.

Owner Phil Checketts has seen the industry change a lot over the years with customers expecting different things from their butcher. He explains, "In the 80s, it was all about people stock-buying meat to put in their freezers. In the 90s, everyone wanted ready meals. Now, it's all about convenience shopping. Customers want a destination shop where they can get everything in one place, but the quality is really important." It's this shift in the way people are shopping that prompted Checketts to diversify their offering, and in 2007 Checketts Fresh Fish Ltd opened up at the back of the shop, but soon moved into the main shop.

Checketts continued to thrive and in 2010, expanded even further taking over the delicatessen and coffee shop next door, and archways were made to create a food hall effect. Phil comments, "Now our customers can come into us and get their meat, fish and cheese. In the coffee shop customers can have a drink or lunch and enjoy the beautiful views from the shop window as they watch the world go by."

And what a beautiful view it is. Nestled in the pretty village of Ombersley, Checketts sits opposite St Andrew's Church and looks onto green fields. It may be a small village, but it's got excellent links to the surrounding areas. "We've got some extremely loyal customers," Phil says. "We don't just serve the Ombersley locals. Our customers travel from neighbouring towns and villages to buy our produce. They appreciate being able to park right outside the shop too. It means they don't have to buy their meat and then carry it all through town."

Considering their customers' needs is something that Checketts excel in. No matter what their customers ask for, they try their very best to source it for them. Phil explains, "My son David is General Manager, and he gets all sorts of requests. He relishes the challenge when customers ask him for specific products, particularly exotic fish from the Indian Ocean. It's a challenge but he always does his best."

And it's this kind of dedication to their customers that's made Checketts famous in the local area. Phil enthuses, "Even though I've been doing this for years, I still love going into the shop in the morning, putting the joints on display, and checking over all the cuts we've had in. I check the quality and if it's not good enough, it's gone. We want our customers to be happy, which makes us happy."

13.

Laurence Wiper

The Regal Cinema

Art deco cinema and live entertainment venue

Business start date
2012

Number of employees
30

Location
Port Street, Evesham

www.theregal.ac

Laurence's business lesson

"If you've got a good idea, just go for it, just make sure you're prepared to work hard. And if anyone tells you that you can't do it, don't listen to them!"

All eyes are on The Regal Cinema following a huge restoration that's transformed the old art deco style cinema into this year's must see!

It's hard to believe that when Laurence Wiper and his family took over The Regal Cinema in 2010, it had been empty and derelict for ten years. But following a huge restoration project the beautiful art deco building, which dates back to the 1930s, now oozes the kind of glamour, sophistication and class of its glory days.

It took a lot of work to bring the badly deteriorated Grade II listed building back to life, but there were a lot of people willing to get involved and help out. Laurence enthuses, "The building is a real Evesham landmark and the cinema is ingrained in local history. It holds a lot of fond memories for the locals and they were keen to see us transform it back into a cinema, rather than watch it get demolished or turned into flats. As such, we had a tremendous level of support from the community. They held fundraisers for us and were more than happy to get their hands dirty and get involved with the building work."

The historical picture palace is now more than just a cinema. Alongside the traditional film showings, The Regal Cinema plays host to a variety of live acts, including comedian Alistair McGowan and musicians Toploader and Nigel Kennedy. Satellite screenings of theatre productions, opera shows and sporting events are also proving very popular.

The building has become a tourist attraction in its own right, with visitors flocking not just to watch a performance on the big screen but to experience the atmosphere and take a look at the original art deco features. "We worked hard during the restoration to keep as many original features as possible," Lawrence says. "We reinstated the architectural details, maximised the fine art deco elements, and furnished the building with comfortable seats, bars and facilities. But without a doubt, the auditorium ceiling and stage area is the focal point. Lots of our customers comment on them."

The Regal Cinema is listed as the number one Trip Advisor attraction for Worcestershire, and Laurence understands the importance of good customer service. He says, "It's a very intimate venue and a personal experience for everyone, we even handwrite our tickets, which means customer service is paramount."

Being in Evesham has had multiple benefits for The Regal Cinema. Laurence comments, "Generally speaking, market towns are usually bereft of cultural elements so our art deco building adds a little something to the area. People also like to support local businesses and are happy to spend their money in their town. Being based in the Wychavon district has also meant that we were able to secure some funding and soft loans from the council at the beginning of the project. They've been very supportive."

There are big plans on the horizon for The Regal Cinema. "We've just secured planning permission to renovate the fourth floor and turn it into two separate screening rooms. We're incredibly excited," Laurence smiles.

MAGNARC

14.

Sarah Vaughan

UK Flood Barriers

Designer, manufacturer and distribution of flood mitigation solutions

Business start date
2007

Number of employees
26

Location
Hampton Lovett

www.ukfloodbarriers.co.uk

Sarah's business lesson

"Be passionate but at the same time dispassionate, this will let you stand back and see your business as a customer does."

When the summer floods of 2007 hit the UK, Sarah Vaughan and her would-be Co-Directors, Frank and Nicky Kelly, witnessed first hand the utter devastation caused by the flooding.

Frank had a background in house building and was keen to incorporate flood-defences into his projects where there was a risk of flooding. The problem was there were very few flood defence products on the market. The solution to this group of entrepreneurs was obvious: they needed to develop their own products and so UK Flood Barriers Ltd was formed.

Sarah Vaughan, the company's Managing Director, says, "The first year or so, from 2007, was all about developing our own product range and we've been developing it and adding to it ever since."

One of the company's products that has made a huge difference to properties within flood risk areas is the Anti-Flood Airbrick, which can be used in new builds but also retro-fitted as a replacement for traditional airbricks that offer no flood protection. A little known fact is that airbricks will let in 5,000 litres of water every hour, and typically houses will have between 12 and 20 airbricks in their outer walls, all of which are set at a low level, often beneath the level of doors.

The clever design, which has been patented, incorporates a flap that is triggered into action and closes the holes whenever water tries to enter the building through the airbrick - and it stays closed for as long as there's water pressure against it. A wire mesh on the outer face of the brick prevents insects and debris getting in and interfering with the mechanism.

Since 2009, the company has grown quickly. It now employs 26 people and is currently looking to recruit further, as it begins to explore and grow new markets at home and abroad. Sarah says, "It's very difficult to quantify the size of the market. Flooding is a global issue and currently there are very few effective engineered flood defence systems available, particularly passive defence systems that require no prior human intervention to activate."

The opportunity for UK Flood Barriers is huge and Sarah is confident that the company's geographical location is a big plus in terms of supporting the business plan. She explains, "We don't just design products and manufacture them here in Worcestershire, we also supply and install them ourselves." She comments, "So in terms of where we're situated, we can get to most areas of the country within four hours. Also we have an abundance of brilliant skill sets in the West Midlands that we've been able to draw on and will continue to draw on, including civil engineers, structural engineers and CAD designers."

UK Flood Barriers is involved in installing their 'Self-Closing Flood Barrier' at the new Bond Street and Liverpool Street underground stations. This particular product works automatically without power or human intervention and with its unique ability to also withstand seismic activity, UK Flood barriers is also working with EDF energy in France to help protect their 19 nuclear plant facilities.

15.

Aidan Stevens

St Andrews Town Hotel

Hotel and 'the dining room' restaurant

Business start date
2012

Number of employees
25

Location
Droitwich Spa

www.st-andrewshotel.com

Aidan's business lesson

"Aim high! Make sure you're not just treading water but that you're developing and growing the business."

When Aidan Stevens was looking for a change of pace, he didn't expect to one day end up running a multi-faceted business that included a hotel, restaurant and wedding venue.

Aidan Stevens's life today is very different to what it was just a few years ago. Working as an investment banker and living with his wife Sarah in London, he stayed in luxurious hotels and made the most of the London restaurant scene. But after the economic downturn, Aidan felt the excitement and vibrancy of the job he once loved had disappeared. He explains, "It was towards the end of 2011 and I just realised I wasn't enjoying my job anymore. The entire industry just felt like it had crumbled and what was once exciting was now tedious and dull and every day was the same."

With his wife's support, Aidan decided to quit his job and started looking for a business they could take over and found themselves drawn to guest houses that could be used as a bed and breakfast. But, after meeting with a mortgage broker, their plans soon changed. "He told me that for the same amount of money we could buy an entire hotel. I initially dismissed the idea as I didn't have any experience in running a hotel, but the more I thought about it, the more I started to warm to the idea. My wife was pretty keen too, so we decided to take the plunge and give it a go," Aidan says.

The husband and wife team started looking for hotels that would offer more than just accommodation. Aidan says, "We were looking for something we could really sink our teeth into, one that had more than just bedrooms. We were thinking along the lines of a restaurant, a bar, meeting rooms and a wedding venue."

Eventually, they decided that St Andrews Town Hotel in Droitwich Spa was the one for them. Aidan explains, "A number of factors were important. We liked Droitwich Spa as a town and all the history behind it. St Andrews as a hotel has always been an important part of local community and we were keen to develop that further. There was a great team of enthusiastic staff already in place who were known for their friendly and personal service, which we felt was really important. And we really liked the creative cuisine of the head chef. In the week, we're usually pretty full of business people because of the close proximity to the M5 and the large number of business parks in the area. On the weekend, it's all about the leisure trade, who like the fact we're so close to the Cotswolds. We hold a lot of weddings here too."

Since taking over the business in the summer of 2012, Aidan and Sarah have increased visitors to the hotel by 15 percent. "We stripped everything back and almost started again. When we first took over the hotel, everything felt disjointed and it seemed like the hotel and restaurant were being run totally separate," Aidan sighs. "The rooms had woodchip on the walls and cost about £45 a night. But then you'd go downstairs and the restaurant was quite formal and charging £18 for good-quality steak and chips. We took our own experience from hotels and restaurants that we've been to and worked hard to bring everything back up-to-date. Now that we've refurbished the hotel and brought the bedrooms up to the same standard as the rest of the building, everything flows much better. My wife's brilliantly creative so the rooms are really quite something!"

"We think the food is one of the big strengths of the hotel, and are keen to encourage local people as well as visitors to come and try our restaurant. We've enjoyed starting to get involved in some of the local events, such as Droitwich's first Food and Drink Festival this year, and were very proud when 'the dining room' won 'Best Local Restaurant'".

It's still early days for Aidan and Sarah but they've got big plans for the future. "We're at the stage where we've invested a lot of money and are just waiting to see what the return is going to be like. Hopefully, there'll be lots more changes taking place over the next few years!"

16.

Steve Cooper

S E Cooper Ironworks

Traditional blacksmith also offering services of an artist, craftsman, ironworker and farrier

Business start date
1989

Number of employees
2

Location
Keytec Business Park,
Pershore

www.stevecooperblacksmith.co.uk

Steve's business lesson

"Always invest your money back into your business, and make sure you work hard. If it's a job you'll love, it won't even feel like working."

Take a walk through the Wychavon district and you're sure to see some of the amazing sculptures that blacksmith and ironworker Steve Cooper has made.

For Steve Cooper, becoming a blacksmith was almost inevitable. Blacksmithing is in his blood, going back five generations from his great grandparents. So it's no real surprise that when he was only ten years old, he'd already made up his mind about what he wanted to do. Steve explains, "My grandfather took me on a trip to see the forge where he used to pump the bellows. That's when I knew that I wanted to become a blacksmith too."

He's come a long way since then. Steve has been a blacksmith in Wychavon for 24 years and is proud of the fact that there's no one else in the area that can do what he does. His work can be seen all around Wychavon, from the swan and fish sculptures in Waterside Gardens to the famous replica whale bones in Workman Gardens. Steve says, "Being commissioned by your local authority and being looked upon as a craftsman is great, and the whale bone sculpture was the biggest commission I've ever done. I'm incredibly proud of it, not just because it's become part of our local history but because it's also given me the chance to leave a legacy for my children and maybe, one day, my grandchildren."

It's an unrivalled passion for his job that's got Steve to where he is today. He's completed two apprenticeships and grown his business into one that specialises in both blacksmith and iron work along with farriery. He's recently completed a five-year Advanced Level Three Apprenticeship to achieve the Diploma of Worshipful Company of Farriers, and he now splits his time between his blacksmith business and assessing, making and fitting of horseshoes.

Managing the two sides of his business isn't easy, especially when dedicated to providing excellent customer service, but Steve makes it work. He explains, "A lot of farriers make the mistake of getting too busy, but that's when you start letting your customers down. I've got a small, but loyal, customer base that I know I can handle. I aim to respond to any enquiries within an hour and unless I'm out on site at a blacksmith job, I'm always available to pay them a visit and fit a shoe."

The business was hit hard during the recession in 2008, but it's a testament to Steve's drive that it's still here today. A sudden decline in orders could have been the end of the business, but some savvy investments and a refusal to give up meant that business soon picked up again. "It's really important not to bury your head in the sand when things get tough," Steve advises. "Wychavon has really supported me as a business. They let me pay my business rates over 12 months instead of ten, which helped a lot with the cash flow. They also gave me a £1,000 grant when we moved into our premises in Pershore Business Park to help us update our IT equipment."

Born and raised in Pershore, Steve couldn't imagine running his business anywhere else. "We're in a great location with wonderful facilities close by, and we've got some of the most beautiful, natural countryside in the country, right on our doorstep," he enthuses. "Plus, the people are fantastic too." In fact, his love for the town he was brought up in is so strong, he recently donated the ironwork railings at Number 8 Community Arts Centre in Pershore, as a way to give something back to the community.

The future's certainly looking bright for S E Cooper Ironworkers and Steve's excited about the challenges ahead of him. He concludes, "The recession nearly took us under but we came out even stronger and to see the business continuing to grow is fantastic. There's no greater feeling than seeing people looking up, admiring and touching your work and having their photograph taken with it. I couldn't think of anything better to be doing, and it gets me out of bed every morning!"

DANGER
HOT SURFACES
BLACKSMITH

17.

Caron Steele

Deer Park

A unique conference and wedding venue plus 10,000 square feet of offices for rent in an area of outstanding natural beauty

Business start date
1999

Number of employees
3

Location
Eckington

www.deerparkhall.co.uk
www.deerparkweddings.co.uk

Caron's business lesson

"Always look at what's going on around you. Things can change very quickly and it's important that you're able to adapt to the changes."

Voted as one of the 'Top Ten Views' in the country by the Guardian, the stunning Deer Park provides an idyllic location for both business and pleasure as it mixes smart office suites and a conference centre with a breathtaking wedding venue.

Life used to be very different for Caron Steele. Before she married her husband Mark and became joint owner of Deer Park, Caron lived and worked in London. "I've worked as an investment banker and more recently, as an Account Director at a global advertising agency. When I got married I continued to commute to London for a little bit, and worked with clients that were based in the Midlands. But I wasn't getting a very good work/life balance, so I decided to go all in and develop a business on our farm estate instead and really start to 'live' in the area."

Her husband's family had successfully farmed the estate for over 40 years, however, there were a couple of farm buildings on the land that were redundant. Caron comments, "We couldn't use them for agriculture purposes anymore, but it seemed a shame to leave them empty because they were such beautiful old buildings made of Cotswold stone. So we set about brainstorming what we could do with them instead."

After doing a lot of research into the local area and seeing what was available, Caron and Mark decided to turn the buildings into office space. "We didn't want to convert them into residential buildings because we didn't really want people living right outside our house. So we settled on offices as an alternative." Caron explains, "We drew up a business plan and did our research about what grants we'd be eligible for and eventually converted the buildings into a suite of 11 offices and a conference centre. The conference centre can also double up as a meeting area for the businesses in the offices, which saves them money. They're able to take out smaller offices because they don't need their own dedicated meeting rooms."

The space currently houses a wide variety of different businesses, from solicitors to occupational therapists and marketing agencies.

Following on from the success of the offices, Deer Park has expanded and is now a popular wedding venue. "It's so important to always evaluate what's going on around you. Initially, we hadn't ever thought about doing weddings. But, during the recession, we noticed a big decline in the number of bookings we were getting for the conference centre," Caron explains. "Businesses were tightening their belts and we really felt it. We needed to come up with a new way to get people coming to Deer Park, and we tentatively agreed to give weddings a go. Now, they're one of our biggest earners and we love doing them!"

It's this passion for what they do that has got Deer Park to where it is today. Caron enthuses, "I really believe that you need to enjoy what you're doing and you need to wholeheartedly believe in what you're doing. That way, when setbacks occur, you can figure out how to get round them rather than throwing the towel in. We had some big obstacles when we first started out and we had to adapt our plans. But I'm so glad we did, because I'm certain that we've got a much better business because of it."

The beautiful countryside certainly helps Caron enjoy her job. She smiles, "Wild horses couldn't drag me away now! I love London but I don't want to move back there. My heart and my business belong in Wychavon."

18.

Clive Brooker

Environet UK Ltd

Eradication of Japanese knotweed – guaranteed

Business start date
1996

Number of employees
6

Location
UK wide with a regional office in Pinvin

www.environetuk.com

Clive's business lesson

"Always continue with your dream and don't stop until you get there, which you will."

When Clive Brooker came across Japanese knotweed during his job in grounds maintenance, he knew he had stumbled across a future career. He just needed other people to see the problem and for him to realise the opportunity.

For those of you not familiar with Japanese knotweed, and therefore curious as to why someone could make a career out of it, here are some of the facts. Japanese knotweed is one of the most invasive plant species in the UK. It is governed by the Wildlife and Countryside Act 1981 and, if found within a residential or commercial property, that property is valued at zero for mortgage purposes. So, it's a serious business and it needs to be dealt with in a serious way that comes guaranteed.

That's where Clive Brooker at Environet UK Ltd gets involved. "When I started to look into the problems associated with Japanese knotweed and realised that it was a growing problem, I found myself getting more and more determined to do something about it. "I definitely had a passion for it and decided to give up my grounds maintenance job to pursue the opportunities I could see in the industry," he explains. "It took over a year to get companies to really understand the seriousness of what I was saying. But when I did get the opportunity, it was to work on the Commonwealth Games, and that's where I proved myself."

A focused determination to keep going at something until it happens is how Clive works. He explains, "When you believe in something so strongly and you know that what you're saying is right, you have to persevere until it happens."

Another high-profile project to add to the list is the London Olympics, where Environet UK Ltd were involved in the regeneration project. "We were approached to provide a rapid and cost-effective answer to the existing problem and we recommended our Xtract™ method, which is designed to remove Japanese knotweed from the infested soil on construction and development sites," Clive explains.

Environet UK Ltd uses either physical removal methods or in-situ treatment methods, depending on whether the land has a development plan or not. "For residential work, we use a herbicide treatment foliar spray three or four times during the growing season from May to September, and we guarantee our work," Clive comments. "I do get real job satisfaction when I'm able to tell a homeowner that it has all been dealt with and they have nothing to worry about. They always say a big thank you."

From Nottingham originally, Clive settled in Pinvin, near Pershore, home to Environet's Midlands' regional office. "I know everyone says the same thing, but it really was a lifestyle choice to settle here. Pershore is a safe and secure place and my children are very happy at the local school," he says. "Being from a big city, I thought the change of scenery might be a struggle, but I really love it here. And I love what I do."

19.

Chris Burdett and Alison King

Stockwood Community Benefit Society Ltd

Farm and business park

Business start date
2013

Number of employees
Shareholders 90+

Location
Stockwood, near Inkberrow

www.stockwoodcbs.org

Chris's business lesson

"Foster your business to help the community grow."

There's a farm and a business park in Stockwood where the strong environmental and ethical principles of its owners are opening up an exciting lifestyle and investment opportunity to residents and the wider community.

The main thrust of the Stockwood and Community Benefit Society (CBS) business is Rush Farm, a working, co-operative organic farm that just so happens to have been the inspiration for the Archers, the long running radio show!

The co-operative farm looks after the land and animals, and investment in the farm is open to anyone who wants to secure it's long-term future and enjoy the outdoors. The other part to Stockwood (CBS) is the business park, which attracts a variety of independent businesses who enjoy the fantastic setting whilst advancing their environmentally sensitive business aims.

To secure the future and protect the principles of the co-op farm and business park for eternity, the family decided to put them into a trust by setting up the Stockwood CBS. Investment in this society is open to everyone, with the opportunity to invest between £100 and £20,000 per member with shares valued at £1 each. How this society differs from many of its kind is that investors can receive returns of up to five percent. So, in addition to the social benefits, there is an opportunity for financial gain, although this is not guaranteed and the focus is primarily on the community benefits this society brings.

Alison King, Company Secretary of Stockwood CBS, comments, "We welcome everyone to the farm and often run open days so that people can experience what goes on. These days are so much more than 'events'. We like people to feel part of the community and encourage them to spend a few hours just relaxing, like they're in their own gardens, seeing where food comes from and taking part in caring for the animals. Shareholders can rent growing lots for just £1 per square metre and grow organically on the farm."

The business park provides office facilities for 15 businesses across 27 units and has an Ofsted approved child care facility. There is a wide mix of different businesses, different styles and sizes of units, from office to light industrial, but all come together to develop a real community spirit.

Chris Burdett, Farm and Business Manager at Stockwood CBS, explains, "Often tenants are able to solve their business problems by co-operating with their neighbouring businesses, which only helps the sense of community. We're often really surprised at just how much they do together."

Share options in Stockwood CBS remain open and exciting times are ahead. Chris concludes, "We want to carry the message that being successful isn't all about making huge profits and owning substantial real estate. Businesses can meet their needs while still achieving social and environmental objectives and benefiting a huge range of people at the same time."

20.

Mick Hurst

Areca Design

Design agency that focuses on new, innovative technologies that help differentiate clients from their competitors

Business start date
2009

Number of employees
8

Location
Abbey Gate, Evesham

www.arecadesign.co.uk

Mick's business lesson

"Take a gradual and steady approach to growth, take your time!"

For Mick Hurst, it's a passion for all things technological that gets him up in the morning, and drives his design business forward.

With a client base built up over several years and a desire to help businesses to differentiate themselves through new, innovative technologies, Mick set up Areca Design in 2009. Mick and his studio team provide design services to businesses, helping to establish a company's look and feel with logo creation, developing promotional materials and coming up with effective e-marketing solutions. It's the digital marketing side that Mick has seen expand significantly in the last few years, thanks to technologies that enable websites to market themselves to search engines, and an increase in demand from clients for more sophisticated e-commerce solutions. And what's brilliant for Mick is that he's never had to advertise. All his business growth has come from word of mouth, referrals and networking.

During year one at Areca Design it was just Mick on his own, getting the business off the ground and building the client base. With a gradual and steady approach to growth (something Mick would encourage others to follow). With a keen eye for innovative technologies, the Evesham-based business now employs eight people and has a client base that spans all corners of the UK.

Servicing local and national businesses, it's Evesham's "smack in the middle" location that has been so beneficial. "Along with the Midlands we have clients in London, Preston, and Devon, and I can reach them all quickly and easily from where we are based. The communication links are excellent," explains Mick. Evesham's close proximity to the countryside was equally important in his decision-making process. Mick highlights, "When you're looking at getting a good work/life balance you can't beat the area. The countryside is literally on my doorstep. Relaxing activities like riding my motorbike and walking my dogs all help with creativity. I couldn't imagine being anywhere else."

As well as growing his own business, Mick enjoys supporting other local businesses through VECTA, the Vale of Evesham Commerce and Tourism Association. “When I moved to Evesham I wanted to do my bit to help the town thrive and being part of VECTA is a good way to help and influence what goes on,” he explains. And in just a few years Mick has already firmly stamped Areca Design’s name (and passion for technology!) on the Evesham history map by bringing the UK’s first ‘Augmented Reality History Trail’ to the town.

Tourists and locals can watch a video created by a combination of real world and computer-generated data just by pointing their smartphone or tablet at one of ten designated buildings, statues or signs on the trail. A mobile monk, who virtually pops up out of the screen, extols a number of fascinating facts to enhance the user’s visit to Evesham. This is just one example of this type of technology and it’s projects of this kind that give Mick confidence and excitement for the future. “The possibilities are endless and I am driven by helping businesses to differentiate themselves through technologies that really enhance creativity,” comments Mick.

Now it’s time to get on his bike and blast around the beautiful Wychavon countryside to keep those creative juices flowing!

21.

Steve Bury

Bury Associates

Surveyors for engineers, architects, town planners and environmental agencies

Business start date
1997

Number of employees
12

Location
Ombersley

www.buryassociates.co.uk

Steve's business lesson

"Don't be afraid to ask your customers for feedback. You'll be able to see what you're doing right or wrong. You'll also be able to use good feedback as testimonials, which will give customers confidence in you."

Say the word 3D to most people, and they'll tell you it's an exciting way to watch films at the cinema. But to Steve Bury, it means so much more.

Established in 1997, Bury Associates is a land and measured building surveyor business that has an extraordinary edge over its competitors. Steve says, "We specialise in creating 3D scans and models of buildings for our customers. We're one of the only businesses in the UK that's skilled in this particular field, and even our closest competitor is about four and a half years behind us."

Taking the decision to expand into the 3D market was a risky one. "It was in 2006 when I started to explore the possibility of investing in the necessary software. Architects create 3D visuals so it made sense for us to supply them with computer-generated 3D visuals, or Building Information Models, instead of the traditional flat drawings," explains Steve. "When we first purchased the software no one really wanted it. We were way ahead of the game but we used that time to make sure we were really up to speed with the complex nature of the software. Now it's gone ballistic and there's a really high demand for Building Information Models. Luckily, we're at the forefront of the industry and so we're really busy."

And being busy is something that Steve relishes. The construction industry was hit hard during the recession, and Bury Associates lost almost 80 percent of its business. Steve explains, "We went from a team of eight to a team of two because we just didn't have the work coming in. It was tough but we survived it, and I'm proud that we've not only come out the other side but we're stronger and busier than ever."

Currently made up of a team of 12, Steve plans to grow Bury Associates over the next few years and is aiming to have a team of 30 people working with him by 2015. "It's a really exciting time for us. We've got some big name clients, such as Lord's Cricket Ground and Manchester Central Library. We also do a lot of work for Merlin Entertainment, who own the Sea Life Centre chain and Alton Towers, among others. Recently we've also worked on Blackpool Tower, which is a great addition to our portfolio."

22.

Marie Handy

Ridgeway Bank Cattery

High-class boarding of cats and most other pets in a safe and secure environment

Business start date
2007

Number of employees
1

Location
Bredon

www.ridgebankcattery.co.uk

Marie's business lesson

"Focus on what might go wrong, that way you're ready to sort it out if it does."

One cat, two dogs, four Shetland ponies and a raft of chickens and ducks. They're the resident pets at Ridgeway Bank Cattery, and there are lots more who just love coming to stay.

It was a lifelong love of animals and six acres of farmland that inspired Marie Handy to set up her cattery. When she and husband Phil bought the farm it came with a small farm shop, but they soon realised the opportunity to open up Ridgeway Bank Cattery, and did so in December 2007 with space for 19 cats. That number soon shot up to 34 and along came a few other animals as well.

Marie explains, "Our initial plan was just for the cattery, but it wasn't long before a regular customer asked if we could possibly take in a couple of pet chickens because she was struggling to find anyone to care for them while she was away. We're surrounded by rural villages where we are in Bredon and many families take the opportunity to have a variety of pets, not just the usual cats, dogs and fish. To meet the needs of our local area, we evolved the cattery into a 'cattery with small pet boarding' and now we look after all types of small pets including rabbits, guinea pigs and hamsters. We also have ten pens dedicated to looking after chickens, which we also breed."

Ridgeway Bank Cattery has very high standards. The pets are treated as individuals and cared for as if they are Marie's own. She comments, "It's funny, but although I can always remember the pet's name, sometimes I do have to ask the owner to remind me of theirs! But they quite like that because it shows that it really is all about the animals." The pets are treated to big, plush surroundings and small animals are kept in pens rather than traditional hutches.

And what about some interesting pet stories? Marie laughs, "We had a tortoise who was obviously enjoying his relaxing stay so much that he decided to go into hibernation, and an African Grey Parrot, called Fifi, who kept us entertained with constant whistling and chatting. There's no way you can be unhappy with a parrot around!"

Business is going brilliantly for Marie. "I've loved every minute of running the cattery but in six years it's been very difficult to take a holiday so I really need to take on my first member of staff and train them up to deliver the same high-quality standards of care that I pride myself on. I suppose, if there is just one downside to running this type of business, it's that you have to plan your holidays around those of your customers!"

23.

Andrew Bille

Evesham Vale Growers

Growers of premium tomatoes, spring onions, courgettes, asparagus and fennel

Business start date
1978

Number of employees
600

Location
Badsey

Andrew's business lesson

"It's all in the detail! Make sure you work hard and concentrate on what you're doing."

It's easy being green for Evesham Vale Growers. And they're looking at new and exciting ways to be even greener in the future.

Andrew Bille knows everything there is to know about tomatoes. From getting the temperature right to watering them little and often, his tomatoes are among the best in the country. And it's no surprise, considering he's at the helm of one of the biggest produce companies in the district, growing premium tomatoes, spring onions, courgettes, asparagus and fennel.

Evesham Vale Growers pack and distribute their produce to supermarkets, catering companies, wholesale markets and food processing companies across the UK, and it all started when Andrew's dad started growing tomatoes with his brother in the 1970s.

There's a strong family ethic running through the heart of the business, which has expanded substantially over the last 40 years. They focus on offering the very best produce to their customers at the best prices possible. Andrew has taken the business down a 'green' route, investing in different technology that not only helps to save costs (that have future-proofed the business), but is also environmentally friendly. He explains, "We plant our tomatoes in January, but they require a temperature of 16 degrees in order for them to grow, so we need to heat the greenhouses. However, this can be expensive. Tackling these kinds of fixed costs is one of the most effective ways to offer our customers value for money, which is why we decided to invest in an anaerobic digester. At a basic level, the digester is powered by a tank that uses old crops and general waste such as chicken feed, which produces a gas that's then converted into energy. We then use this to power the greenhouse."

They've also got a gas upgrading plant on site, which takes the gas that's produced by Evesham Vale Growers and turns it into biomethane. This can then be used to re-heat the greenhouses or injected back into the grid. Andrew says, "By investing in this kind of technology it means our costs are lower, which we can then pass on to our customers. It's made us more competitive, which is great."

The business has always been based in the Evesham area, and it's a location that Andrew can't see them leaving any time soon. And it's not just down to the fact that the soil in the Vale of Evesham is among the most fertile in the UK. He comments, "We're in the middle of the country, which is especially important to us. We can get an order in the morning from someone up in Scotland and the goods can be with them by the evening. It means we're reliable and our customers appreciate that. There's also a great community spirit here, and we try and support as many local businesses as possible."

24.

Enda Spillane

Cocomo Chocolate

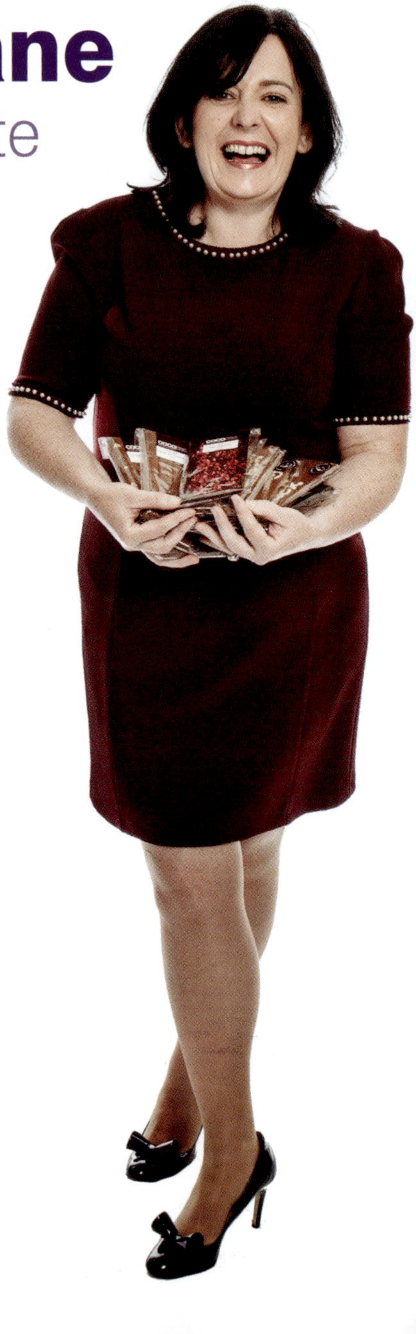

Specialising in high-quality
hand made chocolate

Business start date
2013

Number of employees
3

Location
Stockwood, near Inkberrow

www.cocomochocolate.com

Enda's business lesson

"The harder you work,
the luckier you get."

With a philosophy of encouraging people to buy high-quality chocolate for themselves to enjoy, rather than only buying it as a gift for others (and of course a love of it herself!), Enda Spillane's Cocomo Chocolate is really starting to make a statement.

For someone who has a real desire to turn their passion into their career, there comes a "now or never" moment. For Enda Spillane, that moment happened at the end of 2012, and just three months later, in March 2013, she was up and running with Cocomo Chocolate.

Enda says, "I started experimenting with chocolate when I was self employed working as a marketing consultant, mostly within the IT sector, which was having a difficult time. Chocolate was my idea for a career change as well as a way to achieve my life-long desire to own and run a successful food business." Before being able to set up, Enda had to invest in intensive training and research, which she squeezed into every holiday and spare weekend.

With a background in marketing, Enda wanted her brand to be distinctive, and that's where the penguins came in! She explains, "People generally love penguins. They're friendly creatures and I seem to have found a way to weave them into many marketing campaigns over the years, so I thought why not make them part of my own brand? Our strap line is 'Handmade in Worcestershire by penguins. That's only half true.' It gets people talking and we've had people send in pictures of penguins so they obviously like it."

And people are starting to really like her chocolate too. "Our mission is to show people how to really enjoy chocolate by making sure it's high quality and by helping people to understand how to taste and savour it. Chocolate with a high cocoa content is so much better for you, but you can only eat a little bit at a time," she explains. Popular flavours are marshmallow, fudge and strawberry, dark chilli and, surprisingly, smoky bacon! "It's boys in their late teens and early twenties who always go for this unusual combination," she laughs.

Cocomo Chocolate enjoys a rural location on the Stockwood Business Park, near Inkberrow, and Enda enthuses about the many benefits this location brings to her new business. "To get to work, I drive down this beautiful tree-lined avenue with animals and crops in the fields either side and there's a real feeling of peace and tranquillity," she says. "For us, a rural location is great because people associate it more with artisan production. The business park itself, and the farm, both have a strong sustainable theme and through them we fit in really well, it's perfect for us."

Enda has a motto that she firmly believes in. "The harder I work, the luckier I get," she says with a cheeky smile. "Luck rarely just comes knocking on your door."

25.

Lance Perkins

GuitarStudio

Professional guitar repair and retail

Business start date
2003

Number of employees
1

Location
Fladbury

www.guitarstudio.co.uk

Lance's business lesson

"Be prepared to work seven days a week, 12 hours a day. It'll be worth it in the end."

It's a lucky person who can say they've turned their love into a business, and Lance Perkins is definitely one of them. He spends his days repairing guitars and his evenings rocking out on stage. He even gets to do business with his childhood idols.

GuitarStudio owner Lance Perkins has dealt with some pretty famous faces since opening his guitar repair and retail shop. "It's bizarre when people like Dave Hill from Slade come into GuitarStudio," Lance says. "I used to watch him playing the guitar on the television when I was 12 years old and now he's in my shop, asking for my advice about guitars. It's surreal. Glen Hughes from Deep Purple is a customer of ours too."

Lance has been in his own rock bands since the age of 15, when he first stepped out on stage at Evesham Public Hall as lead guitarist in Medusa. The 35 years that followed have seen Lance play in various different bands such as Wrathchild and more recently, Rockit Fuel, and is currently working on some new material.

Musicians often pop in to GuitarStudio looking for repairs or for help setting up their equipment, and Lance is perfectly placed to offer his expertise. He lives and breathes guitars, and has gone from teaching his friends how to play the guitar in his flat over 20 years ago to completing an apprenticeship in repairing guitars to opening a successful retail and repair shop. He explains, "The business has grown really naturally and at its own pace and I'm really pleased with where I am. Without a doubt, the best part of my job is being able to take old, beaten up guitars that people have found in their loft and restore them to their former glory. It makes it easy to get out of bed in the morning."

Lance is committed to offering excellent customer service, which means that every product that's sold in the shop is tested by him before it's put on the shelf. Lance explains, "I've got experience performing and recording and want to make sure that I fully understand our products. It means I'm better positioned to offer advice and guidance to our customers, which goes down really well."

One day, Lance sees GuitarStudio expanding even further and hopes to eventually be building his own guitars in the next couple of years. "That's the dream. And continuing with my band."

26. Penelope Bossom

Overbury Estate

An estate with a wide range of assets, including agricultural land, woodland, houses, workspaces and community facilities

Business start date
1723

Number of employees
41

Location
Overbury

www.overburyestate.co.uk
www.overburyfarm.co.uk
www.overburygrasshoppers.co.uk

Penelope's business lesson

"Surround yourself with a really good, loyal and happy team, and don't try to do everything yourself!"

Refer to Overbury as a "sleepy rural village" and estate owner Penelope Bossom will beg to differ. A rural village, yes. A sleepy one, not at all.

Behind the distinctive green doors and honey-coloured buildings on the Overbury Estate lies a thriving residential and business community, benefiting from superfast fibre optic broadband, campaigned for and brought to the village by Penelope herself.

Penelope's connection with Overbury Estate, situated on the southern slopes of Bredon Hill, dates back to 1723, when John Martin – of whom Penelope is a direct relative – came to live at Overbury Court. Centuries on, and with each generation having developed particular aspects of Overbury, the estate now has four distinct offerings: Overbury Farms, an arable farm with sheep; Overbury Grasshoppers, a privately owned nursery; Overbury Communications, the superfast fibre-optic service; and Overbury Estate itself, which covers the properties and woodland.

As the buildings and much of the land in and around Overbury are managed by the estate, Penelope has a unique insight into the needs of the residents. "For businesses to consider moving out of a fast-paced city location into a rural environment, they need confidence that their ability to do business, and grow their business, won't be affected by a lack of essential technologies," explains Penelope. "Making sure the estate could provide the superfast broadband necessary was paramount to future-proof Overbury Estate."

So what goes on at Overbury? "The businesses that rent the properties are diverse and dynamic," explains Penelope. "Landscape design consultants, health and safety specialists, school tour organisers and corporate events companies, all enjoying the balance of being surrounded by beautiful and uplifting landscape whilst having access to the technologies needed. Creative industries need fast upload speeds, they need to be able to provide the finished product, be it a film, music or a creative design, to their clients as quickly as they ask for it."

And these businesses enjoy so much else besides. Overbury is really well connected, being just under two hours from London, and the motorway and railway networks allow easy access to the north, south, east and west. It was recently described by a newcomer as "on the way to everywhere" as friends and colleagues just kept "popping in" on their way past.

There's never a quiet moment for Penelope, with new projects on the go all the time. "We are currently building an exciting new school hall and kitchen extension to the village first school," she enthuses. Other projects making the area attractive to families include the Conderton and Overbury Community Orchard. Penelope says, "This part of Wychavon has such a variety of fruit and vegetables; it is so important for children to get involved to really understand where their food comes from and encourage an interest in farming and the environment." The farm regularly hosts schools visits and an annual "Lambing Live" day.

Overbury Estate wouldn't be the well-managed place it is without a strong and loyal team, something Penelope doesn't take for granted. "It's so important to learn from your mistakes and to have a loyal, happy and focused team around you. And always ask for help, don't try to battle on alone."

27.

Malcolm Sunter

Jinney Ring Craft Centre

A real working craft centre with traditional and new crafts all within beautiful old barn buildings, including a restaurant and gardens with duck ponds

Business start date
1980

Number of employees
45+ craft units
20 part-time and full-time

Location
Hanbury

www.jinneyring.co.uk

Malcolm's business lesson

"Recognise that you're on a journey and accept that sometimes you're not going to know where the road will take you."

Set on a quiet country road, between Bromsgrove and Droitwich Spa, The Jinney Ring Craft Centre has unspoilt views of the Malvern Hills. Combine this with delightful craft units and a tasty restaurant and the visitors really have something special to enjoy.

When previous owners Jenny and Richard Greatwood bought Old House Farm, they started The Jinney Ring with just three craft units and a tiny tearoom. Now almost 34 years later and under new ownership, the centre has expanded to 12 craft units, a plant shop, a famed restaurant, plus a wedding and private party venue.

Husband and wife team Malcolm and Amanda Sunter took over the established business in 2005. Malcolm comments, "Jenny and Richard had created a great attraction and really nurtured the Jinney Ring to ensure it kept on growing. When we took over, we knew we needed to keep up the developments and make sure we were offering our customers something new and special."

The range of crafts that take place at the Jinney Ring are wide and varied. Covering everything from glass blowing and chocolate making to skin care and pottery, the centre has become a popular tourist attraction. "We get a lot of coach parties," Malcolm says. "Typically they'll spend the morning with us and have a bit of lunch before they go over to Avoncroft Museum or another local attraction for the afternoon. It means that people are coming to the area for the whole day, which is great. We actively promote these kinds of days out and they go down really well."

The perfect surroundings certainly help the Jinney Ring to stand out from the crowd. Malcolm acknowledges, "Without a doubt, the stunning views out to the Malvern Hills help to bring in the visitors. There are craft centres all over the country but our beautiful views are an attraction in their own right. There's almost no brickwork or concrete to be seen for 20 miles in a straight line. It's spectacular."

Most recently, the Jinney Ring has started to cater for weddings. It's a growing business and one that Malcolm says is very much based on the location. He explains, "We extended the gardens a few years ago so that we could hold wedding receptions here. The views provide a great backdrop for photos and our courtyard looks stunning when it's all decked out for a wedding. It has a very rustic feel, which is very popular."

Talking of popular, there are some very special residents at the Jinney Ring who go down a storm with visitors of all ages. Malcolm laughs, "We have a lot of ducks and our visitors love them!"

28.

Nigel Poole

Nigel Poole and Hancox Estate Agency

Buying, selling and letting of houses

Business start date
1980

Number of employees
8

Location
Evesham and Pershore

www.nigelpooleandhancox.co.uk

Nigel's business lesson

"Do more than just say you give great customer service, really mean it and make a difference."

After gaining a degree in Estate Management in 1976, Nigel Poole went to work for a local estate agency to learn the business. He learned quickly and just four years later he decided that he knew enough to go it alone.

Nigel set up the first of six offices in 1980, and over the next three decades created an enormous business that was responsible for nearly one in three of all properties sold in the area. He employed 65 full and part-time staff and life was good.

In July 2007, with his thoughts already on slowly winding down his commitments to the business, and on when he might actually retire, Nigel and his wife Jan completed the purchase of a house abroad that would enable them to spend more of their 'home time' in a warmer clime.

Almost from that moment on, Nigel and Jan's plans were scrapped, as just two months later Nigel found a lump under his chin, which turned out to be cancerous. Needing a full neck dissection to cut out the cancer, followed by a debilitating course of radiotherapy, Nigel decided his best option was to sell the business.

Nigel found a buyer and a deal was struck, which involved an initial upfront payment, followed by several staged payments over the next few years. However, having bought a successful and thriving business, the new owners found themselves going into administration just one year on. Nigel's 30 years of hard work and more problematically, his pension plan, sustained through staged payments, went out of the window. As if that wasn't enough, at about this time Jan became seriously ill - but thankfully, within a few months, she was able to successfully undergo a heart transplant operation. It had certainly been a traumatic period for the couple in terms of their health and on top of that, they now had no income. Nigel responded in the way that only a great entrepreneur would respond, and that was to go back to work and start again.

In 2010, Nigel opened up again in Evesham with one of his former business associates, Dawn Hancox. An office in Pershore soon followed and they immediately looked at how they could transform the business. With the property market still trying to pull itself out of a recession, they decided that whilst they couldn't be the biggest estate agency from day one, they could be the best, in terms of customer service.

They transformed the service by cutting their fees, opening later in the evenings and on Saturdays and Sundays too with a full complement of staff. They did whatever customers needed them to do every day of the week, from viewings to valuations and everything in between. As Nigel says, "It's very much a customer service thing, but it's also about providing value for money. We spend a lot more on promotion, glossy particulars and bigger adverts. We also have more staff per office than our competitors - to communicate with sellers and buyers and to market the properties properly, as opposed to just putting them in the papers and on the internet."

So what are the plans for the future? Nigel's devotion to customer service dictates that the business strategy is "no more offices, look after the two and look after them well, grow the business from there." This is a strategy that will also enable Nigel to stay close to what he does and loves the best. He explains, "When we had six offices and sixty odd staff, I wasn't doing the job any more, I was just managing people. My love is going in and out of the properties, giving people advice and doing the deals for them, hands on."

29.

Steve Waites

Belle House

Stylish, smart and relaxed restaurant

Business start date
2003

Number of employees
25

Location
Bridge Street, Pershore

www.belle-house.co.uk

Steve's business lesson

"No matter what happens, just keep going."

What more could you want from a restaurant than the promise of locally produced fine food in a relaxed setting? What about the chance to take it home and pretend that you've cooked it yourself?

Belle House opened in 2003 and was taken over by Steve Waites in 2004. Since then, Steve has worked hard to turn it into a premier restaurant that has customers coming from all over the UK. Steve is not just the owner, but the head chef at the restaurant too, and he wanted to create a restaurant that everyone can enjoy. He explains, "We specialise in offering great food in a friendly setting. I didn't want a restaurant that people would be too intimidated to come to. Everyone should be able to enjoy great food, and we're committed to cooking good food and creating a nice atmosphere that people will enjoy eating in."

Set on Pershore's Bridge Street, Belle House specialises in modern Mediterranean-inspired cuisine with a twist. Steve explains, "We use only the best ingredients in our dishes, and we try to source as much local produce as possible. That way, our food not only represents the area but it's also very seasonal, which makes all the difference. We keep our dishes simple, because the flavour does the talking."

Belle House has expanded over recent years and the "creating excellence in food" ethos has taken on a life of its own with the opening of Belle House Traiteur - Deli. The deli is packed full of products that have been made in the Belle House kitchen by Steve and his team. Offering traditional favourites like breads and preserves, the deli also offers customers the chance to buy a range of Belle House specials, including tarts, soups, terrines, cakes and ice cream.

You can even take some of the restaurant away with you. Steve comments, "Time is becoming an increasingly precious thing and many people just don't have the time to make good, wholesome food at home anymore. All of our popular 'take home meals', like lamb tagine, beef bourguignon and fish pie are now available for people to buy from the deli, which makes a great alternative to supermarket ready meals or take aways that are full of additives." The meals come fresh or frozen and are ready to heat and serve, which is perfect when time is limited. Customers can even bring their own dishes to the deli and the team will fill them up. He laughs, "We've had a couple of customers confide that they've managed to pass the meal off as their own because it's been in their own dishes!"

Throughout the year, Belle House Event Catering regularly caters for weddings, parties and events, providing restaurant quality food and a professional service at venues and private homes. They were selected by the event organisers of Posh and Becks' wedding to cater for a large private party in Dorset, and are also nominated caterers at the stunning Deer Park Hall and Stanway House. From canapés for a birthday party to a corporate event or marquee wedding, Belle House are passionate about what they do.

30.

Karen Tomalin

Bras 2 U and Corsets and Cuffs Ltd

Bra sales and flirty accessories

Business start date
Bras 2 U - 2007
Corsets and Cuffs - 2012

Number of employees
5 directors

Location
North Street, Droitwich Spa

www.bras2u.com
www.corsetsandcuffs.com
www.mastectomybras2u.com

Karen's business lesson

"Be determined. Every big organisation starts off small and if you put in enough hard work you'll get to where you want to be. You never know, if you decide to quit, your big break could have been just around the corner."

It's not just the bras that offer support at Bras2U. Owner and director, Karen Tomalin, is the first port of call for ladies in Wychavon who have undergone mastectomy surgery and are looking for someone to give them help post surgery.

"I used to hate shopping for bras," Karen Tomalin says. "It was really hard to find comfortable, flattering lingerie on the High Street and the customer service wasn't very good. It was always a very unpleasant experience." Rather than getting frustrated about it though, Karen went one step further and decided to set up on her own. She laughs, "I decided I could do a better job myself! I knew there were other women who suffered in the same way as me." And with that, Bras2U (formerly 2ndSkinLingerie) was born.

That was back in 2007, and since then the business has grown and grown and she's gone from professionally fitting her friends in her spare bedroom to opening her own shop. Karen explains, "I'm really proud of the shop, it's a nice place to come in and get fitted. When we first started we just did bigger sizes. Then we started to specialise in curvy and shapely underwear before we fell into the mastectomy market." Having previously given away a fitting as a raffle prize, the winner called up to let Karen know that she wasn't able to attend but could she offer the prize to a friend who had recently had a mastectomy. She agreed, and the customer has since become a friend and supporter of Karen and Bras2U. "She inspired me to go off and get trained in mastectomy fitting. It's such a valuable service to someone who has just had surgery and it can really help them."

About 15 percent of the customers that come into Bras2U are women who have had a mastectomy, but it's a number that Karen wants to see drop. "We hope that one day in the future we won't do as many mastectomy bras because a cure will have been found. But until that point we're here to offer a service that's not widely available anywhere else, and we do it because we're passionate about it. We keep our prices low because our ladies need them as a necessity, rather than out of choice." Karen's work hasn't gone unnoticed, she recently became a patron of Worcestershire Breast Unit Appeal.

There's also a saucier side to Karen's business. Hidden away at the back of the shop is Bras2U's sister company, Corsets and Cuffs. Offering customers the chance to pick up some fun and flirty products. The back room is popular with visitors and stocks a range of adult products. Karen laughs, "It's all very tame but it does add an extra element to the business. We get a lot of customers! We call it the '50 Shades of Grey' effect, because the industry has become much more acceptable now. We're very discreet too, which is appreciated."

Every customer that walks through the doors into Bras2U is guaranteed an excellent service and it's one of the things that Karen believes makes them stand out from the crowd. "We have some customers who live abroad and they'll email me to let me know when they're going to be in the UK. Because I have their fitting sheets, I know what kind of styles they like so I can pull together a selection for when they pop in. Bras follow people throughout their lives and it's exciting to be with people as they develop. We'll be fitting someone with everyday bras and then before we know it, we're helping them pick out their wedding underwear! Inevitably, it then follows that we'll be helping with maternity bras and so on. It's a fantastic job and no two days are the same."

Shapewear
Solutions
20% Off
20% Off
Sale

31.

Paul Butler

Rotec Engineering Ltd

Engineering and manufacturing company

Business start date
1995

Number of employees
40

Location
Evesham

www.rotec-ltd.com

Paul's business lesson

"All it takes is knowledge, confidence in yourself, and the willingness to work hard."

Owner of Rotec Engineering Ltd, Paul Butler, has never forgotten his own apprenticeship roots. Which is why he's incredibly proud of his new training academy that specialises in engineering apprenticeships for young people in Wychavon.

Paul Butler is a big believer in apprenticeships. "I started out as an apprentice at a company called Allen Gears in Pershore," Paul says. "I feel so privileged to have been trained by them. They manufacture some very specialist products and they're a really talented team, so it was a great learning experience. They equipped me with so much knowledge and the confidence to branch out on my own and now, 15 years later, Rotec has grown from a one man band to a successful, 40-strong team supplying parts all over the world."

Rotec's extensive manufacturing capabilities mean they're able to manufacture a wide range of precision parts for a variety of industries. "We'll get a call from the F1 team on a Saturday morning and they'll need the parts by Monday. It makes things very exciting! Luckily, not all our customers require such a fast turnaround," explains Paul. "One week we'll be manufacturing automotive parts for Jaguar Land Rover, the next we'll be producing ground support and fire fighting equipment and extinguishers for the Ministry of Defence, and then we're providing components to the packaging industry. Because we work with so many varied industries the work we do is never the same."

Thinking back to his time as an apprentice, Paul comments on how there were only three other apprentices in his year, and that the true worth of their experience can be seen, given they're all now running their own successful manufacturing businesses in the local area. "I want to be able to give other young people the same kind of opportunities that I had. That's why we've opened our training academy," he says.

"If every year we train about 15 new apprentices, and even if just a few of those go on to open their own business, then I'll be very proud. I've worked hard to get where I am today, which is why our apprenticeships don't just focus on teaching our students about engineering. We also teach them about the commercial side of running a business and try to instil a good work ethic in them."

Paul's definitely a great person to demonstrate how working hard and having faith in yourself can be the key to success in business. A few years after setting up the business, he took the decision to invest in an expensive piece of computer numerical control equipment that he knew would benefit Rotec. But it cost more than his house to buy and raising the money was difficult. However, when he finally made the purchase it was a defining point for the company. Paul explains, "I realised that investing back in the company was the only way to keep it moving forward and since then, we've always strived to buy the best equipment available. It means we're able to provide an excellent service to our customers and our products are high quality."

32.

John Fisher

Recent and Rare Records

Record shop and online store dealing in collectable music, including records and tapes

Business start date
1991

Number of employees
1

Location
Bridge Street, Evesham

www.recentandrarerecords.com

John's business lesson

"Don't be afraid to try something new and if it doesn't work straight away, try it again in the future."

Walk into John Fisher's record shop in Evesham and be prepared for a shop full of stories and some intriguing vinyl-related facts along the way!

Recent and Rare Records started life on Pershore Market in 1991. Just two weeks in and the offer of a "van full of records for £400" was too good a deal to pass up. Crate after crate of vinyl kept John busy and the more he delved, the more opportunities he found, and the more excited he became.

One unique aspect about John's business is that he often finds himself selling his product back to its creator, and not many people can say that! Sonny Curtis of the Crickets and country singer Jimmy Rodgers (who still sends John a Christmas card every year) are just two of John's customers who've sought out Recent and Rare Records to acquire specific editions of their own work. His most prized possession, and the rarest record he owns, is a collaboration between Sid Vicious, Chrissie Hynde and Steve Strange when they were managed by Malcolm McLaren. People travel far and wide to visit John's shop and the records can then travel even further to their new owners, often overseas.

Another famous name close to John's heart and business is Miss Billie Davis. A sixties starlet with hits including 'Tell Him' and 'I Want You To Be My Baby', Billie has been a big supporter of John's business over the years and John now manages Billie, and her fan club.

With 22 years behind him as owner of Recent and Rare Records, John knows what has worked for him. "You've got to try new things," he explains. "They won't always work first time, so put them to one side and get on with something else, but never disregard them completely because there will be a time in the future when they do work."

Saying that John has a "passion for the industry" is just not descriptive enough, it only scratches the surface. Recent and Rare Records is a thriving business today because John stands by his love of vinyl. He never undersells. "If you really know your customers then you can spot the ones who share the same love of records and who will place the same value on the rare ones," John explains. "Nowadays, people come into the shop expecting everything to be 10p - they think a dying industry will be selling off cheap," he says. "But I can spot the people who are really hoping to find something special, and they're the ones I spend time with to make sure they go away happy."

Who says it's a dying industry? Certainly not John! "In 2001, Britain's oldest vinyl pressing plant, the EMI factory in Hayes, was in the process of being sold off to developers, but they had a change of heart and pledged to keep it as it was. It's now a flourishing business," highlights John.

"Vinyl has a certain feel, a certain smell – it's just so good to hold," he says. "There's really nothing else like it."

33.

Joe Pilade and Vito Mauro

Valefresco

Growers of leaf vegetables, salads and tomatoes

Business start date
2006

Number of employees
30 permanent
150+ in high season

Location
Offenham

www.valefresco.com

Joe and Vito's business lesson

"Always look for the next innovation, the next big product that can help grow your business."

If you're looking for continental salads, baby leaf and oriental vegetables, then take a trip to Valefresco in Evesham, where two families, both with 25 years' experience, are continuing to offer a wide range of delicious products at competitive prices.

It was in 2006 that the families behind the growers V&S Pilade and G&G Mauro - both sharing the same quality-led philosophy - decided to pool resources and knowledge to create a new and dynamic community. Valefresco was born and with it came a real determination to invest in new products and new technologies, particularly ones that help extend the growing season, improve freshness and reduce their carbon footprint.

The business has continued to go from strength to strength and is now jointly owned by the founding fathers' sons, Joe Pilade and Vito Mauro Jnr. "Both V&S Pilade and G&G Mauro were strong family businesses," Vito explains. "My father Vito came over to the UK in the late 1960s to work on farms and then we all helped out as children where we could, and Joe's family did the same. So you can definitely say we're following in our fathers' footsteps."

When their fathers first came to England, they concentrated on growing traditional English vegetables, but as the nation's tastes changed, they've further extended their offering to keep up with the demand for Chinese food. Valefresco is now at the heart of the UK oriental vegetable industry, but it wasn't always that way.

Joe comments, "We first turned our hand to producing oriental vegetables about 25 years ago. A Chinese man knocked on our door with a selection of seeds and asked if we would like to plant them. We gave it a go but they didn't sell very well. Consumers just weren't ready for them back then. Since then, the market's changed quite a lot. About ten years later the same man turned up at our door again. We gave it another go and we haven't looked back since." Now, they've got greenhouses filled with vegetables like pak choi and Chinese cabbage and supply Chinatowns all over the UK.

The Valefresco workforce fluctuates with 30 permanent employees in winter, it rockets up to 150 in the main season. "It's like a big family in summer," says Vito. "Our temporary staff are well looked after and they come back to work for us year after year."

And a good summer means a busy time for the company. Valefresco's best-selling lines are their specialist lettuces such as Lollo Rossa, Course, Fine Endive and Cos. "We specialise in leafy produce such as whole-head lettuce, multi-leaf lettuce and baby leaf. All are grown on demand, especially in summer, where sales of salads through retailers and caterers increase dramatically."

34.

Karen Drinkwater

JSC Rotational Ltd

Manufacturers of rotational mouldings

Business start date
2003

Number of employees
35

Location
Inkberrow

www.jscrotational.co.uk

Karen's business lesson

"Don't be happy with standing still, strive to be the best at whatever you're doing."

There's a whole load of plastic going on down at a family farm in Inkberrow and Karen Drinkwater, along with husband and business partner Mark, are the ones to fill us in on their hollow plastic specialities.

When Karen Drinkwater of JSC Rotational Ltd explains what it is that her company manufactures, she usually ends up saying that if it's large, hollow and made from plastic, then it's probably a rotational moulding - or rotomoulding to coin another industry term.

JSC Rotational was founded in October 2003, and by March 2004, the company had started manufacturing. Karen had held senior positions in contract packing and logistics, whereas husband Mark came from the polymers industry, so together they had the technical, production and managerial experience to set-up, using the family farm in Inkberrow as their premises. They didn't want to be farmers, but didn't want to lose the family farm either.

In what is quite a niche market, with only around 60 rotomoulding companies in the UK, JSC Rotational wants to be the best at what it does. "We've got the technical capability and production know-how to make a vast range of products, but we want to be one step ahead, we want to be continually suggesting new ideas and opportunities to our customers," explains Karen.

Go about your everyday business and you'll probably walk past something made by JSC Rotational. From baby-changing stations, horse jumps and car parts to ice cream litter bins and free-standing hand-wash facilities, JSC pretty much does it all. Oh, and not forgetting the green bins that you see next to the tennis players on centre court at Wimbledon when they're having a quick sit down between games! They're made in Wychavon too.

Karen continues, "Rotomoulded items are weather-resistant, robust and very versatile, and they can be manufactured in vivid colours. One of our latest developments is the Scooterpod, for www.cyclepods.co.uk. It's a mushroom-shaped hollow plastic scooter rack that we supply to nurseries and primary schools. It's fun, bright and holds up to 12 scooters."

Bringing innovation to the sector is what Karen and Mark are really focusing on, and it gets them closer to their goal of being the best in the industry. "We work closely with our customers on product development - we're definitely more of a partner than just a supplier." Karen explains, "Niftylift makes cherry pickers and work platforms and they were looking to replace the metal floor of their cages with a plastic option to reduce material cost and weight without compromising quality. They now have a solution using rotational moulding that gives them a competitive advantage because their cherry pickers can reach higher as a result of the weight reduction. Our technical expertise combined with their design knowledge helped deliver exactly what was needed."

Setting up in business was "the best thing we ever did" according to Karen, but she does stress that it doesn't just happen overnight. "You've really got to be prepared for hard work and you need to plan out all aspects of what you hope to achieve," she says. "And you never really get there either because, if you're anything like Mark and me, you're always looking for the next challenge to make sure your company is ahead of the game and coming up with the next new and exciting thing."

And what does JSC stand for? Karen explains, "We've named the business after our children Jonathan, Stephanie and Charlotte, to reflect how important they and the business are to us." And with recent coverage in The Sunday Times, sharing their story and research work with Warwick University, life in plastic is looking good for the future.

35.

Dale Parmenter

DRP Group

Specialising in events, video production, digital media, design and print

Business start date
1980

Number of employees
135

Location
Hartlebury

www.drpgroup.com

Dale's business lesson

"Look after your people and trust them."

Dale Parmenter's video and events management business is a long way from where he started out, based in a shed in his parents' back garden, growing and selling Christmas trees and tomatoes.

But Dale quickly learnt that he had skills in video making and started using the shed as an editing studio instead. He soon won some bigger clients like carpet giant Brintons and the business grew from there.

The secret of Dale's business is getting the right people. Dale elaborates, "We employ 135 people and all of them are control freaks! All they want to do is be in there with their client from concept to delivery getting it right.

"Having the right people to make things possible, trusting them and having an open organisation is what has helped us become one of the top ten service agencies in the UK today, something we've won a lot of accolades for."

And the Group's list of accolades is extensive, from The Sunday Times Top 100 Best Small Company to Work for, to Investors in People Gold status and Best Service Agency, to name just a few.

The company is also unique, specialising in events, video production, digital media, design and print, and team building, which is of great benefit to their customers. This is because they keep control over all aspects of the projects and don't have to sub-contract work.

They work for an extensive client list as well with big brands like Sainsbury's, Thomas Cook, Lloyds Banking Group, JCB and Worcester Bosch all coming back for more of this first class service.

Dale also has a lot of positives to say about the area. "We moved to the Ikon Estate from Bewdley in 1989. It's a wonderful location to do business, there are great links, it's tucked away, clients love that it's peaceful and quiet, and we can be flexible in terms of what we can do there."

36.

Ed Webb

Webbs Garden Centre

Award-winning, family-run garden centres with over 150 years' horticultural pedigree

Business start date
1850s

Number of employees
280

Location
Wychbold

www.webbs.co.uk

Ed's business lesson

"Understand the evolution of business and know when to step back to give others the confidence to develop and grow."

For a family business that goes back so many years, centuries even, it seems only right to tell the story from the very beginning. And who better to do this than Chairman, and fifth-generation family member, Ed Webb.

Mention Webbs of Wychbold to anyone from Wychavon and they'll know all about it. They'll know where it is and they'll probably have been there at least once in their life. But this family-run garden centre, lifestyle and leisure business is also well-known outside of the area – it's a destination place and is even signposted from the M5!

It all started back in the 1850s when Edward Webb was a successful agricultural seeds merchant trading in the Stourbridge area, in the West Midlands. Edward's grandson, William, took over the business in the early 1900s, which was by then well established, and involvement in the Wychbold area began with the purchase of Astwood Farm in 1925, before moving to the company's current A38 location in Wychbold in 1937.

When the English seed trade was transformed by a series of mergers in the 1960s and 70s, the Wychbold site focused its attentions on becoming a garden centre, under the leadership of William's son Michael. Then in 1971, Richard Webb, great grandson of the original Edward Webb, purchased the site from his uncle Michael and so began the development of Webbs as both a garden centre and nursery. From then on, Webbs has established itself as a leading horticultural centre and regional tourist attraction and today the business is led by Ed Webb, great, great grandson of the firm's founder.

"The Webb family has indeed ploughed blood, sweat, energy and tears, in addition to dirty finger nails, into this business to make it what it is today," explains Ed. "The family essence of Webbs of Wychbold is so strong, it runs across every aspect of what we do."

Today, Webbs of Wychbold today is a flagship for garden centres around the world. It's a place where people can spend a few hours surrounded by products and services that fit perfectly with their lifestyle interests in a relaxed environment with attentive service. "People who enjoy gardening often have an active lifestyle. They enjoy getting out and walking and they have a keen interest in all aspects of food - growing it, nurturing it and then cooking," explains Ed. "We cater for our gardening, lifestyle and leisure customers in the very best way possible."

The Webbs Group has over 300 employees at two sites in the Midlands: the Wychbold Garden Centre, and a second in West Hagley. The company also has part ownership of a horticultural business in Malvern that grows 4.5 million plants every year and employs 60 people.

Although Webbs of Wychbold is a mature business, there's always something new to experience. In 2013, they introduced 15 hives for honey bees and at the time of writing, 900 jars of their own honey have been produced. The evolving nature of the business is what really excites Ed. He comments, "I can honestly say that I love the changing pace of retail. It's not something that frustrates me or gets me down - I'm always keen for the challenge and ready to look for the best way to adapt, or more importantly, get ahead. It's this constant need for change that brings out my entrepreneurial side and I love every minute."

37.

Viv Hudson

Hotelshop UK Ltd

Hotel specialists for both the leisure and corporate sectors

Business start date
1999

Number of employees
48

Location
Tower Hill, Droitwich Spa

www.hotelshopuk.com
www.greatlittlebreaks.com

Viv's business lesson

"Spot opportunities and try new things, and always do it with a bright and positive outlook."

Being made redundant for the second time from director-level positions within the hotel trade made Viv Hudson question whether she really wanted to stay in the corporate world. She decided to go it alone and soon after, Hotelshop UK opened for business.

It was in October 1999, with 16 years experience gained with Forte Hotels and seven years at Corus Regal, that Viv Hudson launched Hotelshop from retail premises on Droitwich Spa High Street. With excellent contacts at all the hotel groups in the UK and an in-depth understanding of the industry, Viv set out to delight customers with all aspects of their hotel bookings. Business was going strong and growing steadily when, in 2007, Hotelshop was a major victim of the floods, as were many other businesses in Droitwich Spa.

Viv recounts, "In summary, we were completely wiped out. Hotelshop was 12 feet under water and our recently installed computer backup system didn't work. We lost absolutely everything, every single customer record that we had built up over eight years." But Viv's resilience and ethos of always having a bright outlook soon paid off. With support from the business community, including a loan of laptop's to help keep customer contact going, Viv and the Hotelshop team were resettled and fully functional in new office premises just five weeks later.

The devastating situation caused by the floods was the start of a new direction for the business. In keeping with the changing nature of hotel bookings, Viv decided to focus Hotelshop's attentions online. "I saw this as an opportunity to grow the business and establish a strong website presence that would allow people to search for and book our packages and special offers online.

Last year, we expanded our service even further and now partner with over 100 insurance companies to help place flood victims in emergency hotel accommodation, which requires us to offer a 24/7 call centre," she explains. "There are 48 of us working from our Droitwich Spa offices, and this may soon increase if a couple of big new contracts come good."

Investing in the business, and the people, is something that Viv has done from day one. "I've always ploughed profits back into Hotelshop to ensure stability and facilitate growth. I've still got very ambitious growth plans and to achieve these, I need the best team," says Viv. "Some of my most senior employees started out in the call centre back in 1999, and it's great to see local talent develop through the company. Our clients like speaking to the same person every time they book - they love the personal service and are very thankful. It's not uncommon for bunches of flowers to arrive when one of the team has obviously gone the extra mile to make sure a special occasion is extra special."

As well as her love for her job, Viv's passion for the area is clear to see. Although Newcastle is her home town, she says that her heart is in Worcestershire, having moved there 30 years ago. "Personally I love the area, and with my business hat on I'm actually selling more hotels in Worcestershire than I've ever done in the last 14 years. There are some excellent hotels with very high-quality restaurants and nobody can be more passionate about selling an area than someone who lives there!"

38.

Ken Bryant

Chase Heating Ltd

Suppliers of high quality, wood-burning stoves, range cookers and biomass boiler systems

Business start date
1969

Number of employees
5

Location
Racecourse Road, Pershore

www.chaseheating.co.uk

Ken's business lesson

"Work as hard as you can, and you'll get where you want to go."

Chase Heating has been 'warming the hearts of the local community since 1969' with its high-quality, wood-burning stoves and flue systems. Owner Ken Bryant knows all there is to know about the industry, and he's about to embark on a new 'green' venture.

The demand for wood-burning stoves has been on the up in recent years with homeowners increasingly appreciating the cosy appealing look and feel of a fire. But increasingly there is a developing market for wood as a renewable energy source. For Ken Bryant, wood-burning stoves and flue systems have been his daily life since purchasing the business in 2001. Back then, Chase Heating was based in Head Street, Pershore. In 2007, Ken took the decision to move to a unit in Racecourse Road, which is now the company's well-established office and retail showroom.

Ken explains, "We kitted out the premises with a variety of in-situ displays of wood-burners so that customers could get a really good feel for how our products might look in their home. Since moving here in 2007, we've had some really good years. The recession has been a bit difficult and there's no doubt that internet sales have taken their toll, but our products are in demand and we do have repeat customers, including those that travel up and down the motorways to see us."

Soon Chase Heating's customers will have a new range of energy-efficient boilers to consider for their home heating as well. "It's an exciting new venture for us," says Ken. "We're going to be an approved dealer for a Seattle-based manufacturer, Greenwood Clean Energy, who are making the next generation of wood-burning boilers for residential and light commercial use. The UK has been identified as a promising market for these 'green' systems and once the products are certified, they'll be eligible for subsidies under the Government's Renewable Heat Incentive Scheme."

In addition to bringing this new venture to Wychavon, Ken has also helped to secure work for a neighbouring business that will be manufacturing components not only for the Greenwood boilers sold in the UK but also for those planned for sale in the US. Ken comments, "Greenwood have a mission to fill their returning 'empty' shipping containers with goods from the UK, and one product group definitely on the list will be the components made by fellow Racecourse Road company Mechanical and Pipework Fabrications.

Logistically, Pershore is ideally placed for the transportation aspect, but also for the potential new business. There are many farms that have easy access to big logs, and they're what's needed to burn and turn into energy, so it's good news all around."

Pershore born and bred, Ken does everything he can to support the local economy. "I endeavour to employ local people where possible and am always on the look out to put local companies forward where there's a chance of work. Many of my employees went to Pershore High School and I went there too," he comments. "I didn't work as hard as I could have done at school, but I always tell people that I wish I had. Hard work is what gets you through in life, as long as you're working as hard as you can, you'll get where you want to go."

39.

Kit Bamford

Kit's Kitchen

Award winning chef, creating unique dressings, chutneys and pickles in partnership with a local farming family

Business start date
2003

Number of employees
2 staff and 3 partners

Location
Egdon

www.kitskitchen.co.uk

Kit's business lesson

"Know your products, understand your costs and research your route to market really well."

When chef Kit Bamford got chatting to two farmers, Tim and Colin, about an ancient chutney recipe in his local pub, he knew he'd struck gold. And a few years later he proved it with a Gold 'Great Taste' Award.

As an award-winning chef with an established catering business in Worcestershire, Kit Bamford was well placed to try out an old apple and onion chutney recipe that dated back to 1880. Add to that jars of pickled shallots and Kit's Kitchen was born. The business, which officially got off the ground in 2003, is a three-way partnership between Kit, Tim and Colin who provide many of the tasty, local ingredients.

Between them they've created a range of top quality, homemade food accompaniments that have made it onto the shelves of Selfridges in Birmingham and are readily available in Warner Budgens stores across the region.

Kit's Kitchen sources locally wherever possible. Kit explains, "Real care and attention goes into our chutneys and accompaniments. We use as many local ingredients as possible, I can even tell you which field the beans came from in our Runner Bean Chutney!"

It's by having such a strong passion for flavours and textures, and with access to such a variety of produce, that has won Kit so many 'Great Taste' Awards. Most recently a Gold two star award for the apple juice and a Gold one star award for the cider. He explains, "Our Naked Apple Juice and Nearly Naked Cider came about because the farmers had an abundance of apples. We got them pressed up at Pershore College and bottled the juice straight from the press, with nothing added. Then we added a bit of sugar and yeast to the leftover juice and made cider. It was as simple as that, and we achieved two Gold 'Great Taste' Awards. We're obviously doing something right!"

And Kit's Kitchen's customers think so too. "Our customers are always keen to give us feedback, they send letters and emails telling us what they like and what they'd like to see us produce," says Kit. "Our pickled shallots are a real winner, we send case loads to a customer in Wales on a regular basis, and we're seeing people's palates changing. There's big demand for more spicy accompaniments at the moment, such as chilli jams and onion marmalades."

"Because of where we're based, close to the motorway network, we've managed to work out a cost-effective and environmentally friendly way of getting our products to our main distributors," Kit adds, "We use a back haulage system, which means that empty lorries, on their return journeys, pick up from us and take to our distributors."

Clever thinking and a real understanding of products, costings and route to market have helped Kit to build a thriving business. "You've also got to ask for help," adds Kit. "Take advice where you can. I've always worked well with Wychavon's environmental health officers who I know can help me to get ahead of where I need to be, which will help me to grow my business. I was just a beginner twelve years ago and now I'm running a thriving business that I love."

40.

Bob Pooler

Roundabout

A charity that collects unwanted furniture and makes it available for people encountering hard times

Business start date
1994

Number of employees
4
40+ volunteers

Location
Blackminster Business Park, Evesham

www.roundaboutevesham.org.uk

Bob's business lesson

"Grow steadily and focus on building your contacts for a long-term future."

Giving unwanted furniture to families and individuals in need is what the charity, Roundabout, is all about. Bob Pooler and the team have been doing it for nearly 20 years.

The work that goes on at Roundabout, in Evesham, is vital, not only for the recipients of the donated furniture but for the volunteer community as well. Manager Bob Pooler explains, "We source unwanted donated furniture from residences and commercial properties and then make it available to people in need that have been referred to us via agents within care agencies. Our warehouse is also open to the public, who can purchase furniture at a reasonable price, which helps to provide funds to keep the charity viable."

There are obvious environmental and economical benefits to Roundabout but there are social ones too, and the charity is equally loved by its employees and volunteers as it is by its beneficiaries. Bob continues, "We have more than 40 volunteers, many longstanding, including people with learning difficulties. For them, Roundabout provides both a mental and physical challenge in a relaxed working environment, something they might struggle to achieve in a typical workplace.

Centrally located in Evesham, Roundabout has the advantage of being able to tap into opportunities from the three counties of Worcestershire, Gloucestershire and Warwickshire, and Bob and the team have received donations from big local organisations, including G4S and the Fire College in Moreton-in-Marsh. "We've been in Evesham since 1994 and have moved three times, each time to slightly bigger premises to give us the extra space needed," explains Bob.

"It's always been my philosophy to grow Roundabout modestly, a little each year, and to spread our sources so that we don't rely on just a few donation streams. I'd love to think that some time in the future, we might have access to purpose-built premises that would allow us to display our furniture more appropriately, and in a way that is better suited to the needs of our customers," says Bob.

ROUNDABOUT
ROUNDABOUT
www.roundaboutevesham.org.uk
Tel: 01386 83 30 30
ROUNDABOUT
Manager

41.

Fiona Roberts and Gillian Kerton

Churchfields Farmhouse Ice Cream

Award winning producers of high-quality, traditionally made ice cream

Business start date
2003

Number of employees
3

Location
Salwarpe

www.churchfields-farm.co.uk

Fiona and Gillian's business lesson

"Recognise that it's not just about how much you sell, but it's also about your gross margins. If you're selling lots of product but your profit margins are low you'll be really busy without seeing any results."

Ice cream isn't just for enjoying on the beach on a sunny day. Churchfields Farmhouse Ice Cream sell their award-winning ice cream all year round, all over Wychavon and beyond!

In the aftermath of foot and mouth disease and with plummeting milk prices, the Davies family knew they needed to shake up their dairy farm in order to survive. And with that, Churchfields Farmhouse Ice Cream was born. Gillian comments, "Our grandfather bought the farm in 1913 and we were determined not to lose it. With our skill-set, premises, resources and interest, ice cream production seemed a viable way for us to diversify the farm."

The decision has certainly paid off. Together with her parents, Gillian Kerton has been producing and selling their ice cream for ten years. Gillian's sister, Fiona, returned home two years ago as the business grew, and the two sisters now work together. It's not just during the summer months either. Churchfields Ice Cream is sold in a variety of pubs and restaurants in the local area, and the sisters' distinctive green ice cream trike is a regular at events and shows. Fiona explains, "The great thing about ice cream is that it's an affordable luxury. People can still afford to treat their kids to an ice cream at the park or indulge in one at a festival. We've found that when we've attended shows, people can't always afford to make big purchases but they can always find a bit in their budget to treat themselves to some ice cream. The appetite is always there for high-quality, good tasting ice cream."

And good-quality it is. Churchfields has won a whole host of awards for their ice cream, and they're proud of their achievements. "We've defined our place in the market through the awards we've won. We pride ourselves on the fact we use traditional methods to make ice cream, which separates us from our competitors and our customers love the delicious range of flavours that are available too," enthuses Fiona.

From the traditional to the outrageous, Churchfields Ice Cream have a flavour for everyone. "We did a Seriously Stilton flavour a few years ago," Fiona explains. "It was a great PR opportunity for us and we were in every national newspaper in the country. Not surprisingly though, we didn't sell much of it! Caramel is always really popular and sells incredibly well. To tie in with the 2012 Olympics we created a caramel, honeycomb and fudge flavour, which we called Going for Gold. We had such a great reaction to it that we've kept it as a permanent flavour but changed the name to Gold Rush as a tribute to the fantastic amount of gold medals Team GB won. We also created a Popping Penguin flavour for Dudley Zoo to mark the opening of their new penguin enclosure, which was a wonderful event to get involved in."

Where possible the sisters make sure to source their ingredients locally, and you can't get much more local than the plums that are used in the new Worcester Plum ice cream - they come straight from Gillian's back garden. "Our customers understand the importance of supporting local businesses and enjoy buying locally-produced products. The rural nature of our farm means we get a lot of support and loyalty from the local community, which has really helped our business grow."

Fiona used to work in politics before she got involved in the ice cream trade, and admits she used to dread Monday mornings, but things are different now, she's working with her family in a successful family business. "I love Mondays now," claims Fiona, "They're my favourite day of the week!"

Stop me and buy one !
Dairy Ice Cream
Churchfields farmhouse
Ice cream
"Homemade on the farm with milk from our pedigree herd"
Freshly made
just for you !

42.

Phil Marsay-Jones

Cepha Controls Ltd

Providing custom-made automation and control solutions

Business start date
1996

Number of employees
13

Location
Droitwich Spa

www.cepha.co.uk

Phil's business lesson

"Start small and grow organically. There's less risk that way."

Phil Marsay-Jones is an engineer who loves to make things work. And that's exactly what his company, Cepha Controls Ltd, is doing for businesses all over the world.

Cepha Controls has been designing, developing and commissioning control systems for industrial processes for almost 20 years. From sewage treatment plants to car manufacturers, Phil Marsay-Jones and his team have experience in it all. "In a nutshell, we're engineers and we make things work. We provide electronic control solutions to a variety of industries, but we specialise in the water and waste treatment industry, where we develop processes that clean water and make it fit for drinking," he explains.

Phil set up the company in 1996 as a sole trader, but since then Cepha Controls has expanded to 13 members of staff, who work on projects across the globe. He comments, "We recently went to Iraq to look at the water treatment processes of four plants out there to help bring their standards up to Western specification. We've also worked on projects in Brazil and we do a lot over in America too."

Despite working with clients in such far-flung locations, Phil has no plans to relocate the business anywhere else. "I love being based in Droitwich Spa," smiles Phil. "We're on the edge of the industrial heartland of England! Plus, being so close to Birmingham airport has its advantages when we have to travel to meet our clients." It helps that his office is in a beautiful old Georgian townhouse too. He enthuses, "Our office is great. When I first started working it was in an old building that had no windows and it was pretty uninspiring. I made a pact with myself that I didn't ever want to end up working in an industrial unit again and when I found our current offices I just thought they were perfect."

With engineering at the heart of the company, Phil and his team work hard to make sure the control solutions they provide their clients are exactly as they need them. "We have some tough competition and there are a lot of people out there who do what we do. What separates us from them is our complete dedication to our clients," he says. "It's one thing to create a control solution that works in a perfect world, but it's completely different to one that works in the real world. We make sure all of our solutions work."

Phil's excited about what the future holds for the company. "There are some really interesting developments happening in the industry at the moment and we're right in the thick of it. We've been signed up to develop a control system that will essentially take household waste and turn it into energy. We can't wait to get started."

43.

Victoria Poole

Poole Phillips Associates

Architects specialising in conservation, sustainable design, interiors and lighting design

Business start date
1993

Number of employees
7

Location
High Street, Pershore

www.poolephillips.co.uk

Victoria's business lesson

"We set up in a recession and the economy was down 2%, but that still gave us 98% to go at!"

With local, national and international clients on their books and award-winning conservation work on their list of accolades, it's no wonder architects Poole Phillips Associates celebrated 20 successful years in business in 2013.

"Twenty years is a long time and although lots of things have changed, I'm also pleased to say that many things are still the same," explains Victoria Poole, architect and co-founder/owner of Poole Phillips Associates. "We're still based in our versatile High Street location in Pershore, we've still got a strong, loyal team and we still do work for some of our very first clients!"

In the early 1990s, during a recession, Victoria and business partner Paul were in the process of setting up on their own when an opportunity to work in Jeddah for a Saudi princess came along. This might sound like a fairy tale but it turned into a huge success story and the initial project, working on the head office of a travel agency, then evolved into looking after the development of a number of outlets. It didn't stop there. Poole Phillips impressed so much that they were soon working on the Sheikh's Suites followed by a private apartment in London. Fifteen years on and they've been asked to manage a major refit of the apartment. "I love the variety of being an architect, but what I also love is when a client comes back to you, and when they refer you on as well," Victoria comments.

State-of-the-art BIM computer software, used for modelling buildings in 3D, is one of the aspects that sets Poole Phillips apart from its competitors. "We've been using techniques like this for about seven years now, and we were definitely one of the earliest adopters of this approach in the UK," explains Victoria. "We're probably in a handful of practices that have the capacity to do conservation or restoration work using this highly technical system."

Victoria's specialism is conservation and she also has a developing interest in sustainable design. A current project has required Poole Phillips to work on an eco home in Worcestershire. "The plot of land was very tight, so we had to think of different ways to deliver the space and aspects much-desired by the client," she comments. "By turning our thinking, and the house, upside down so that they park on the roof and enter the house via a downwards spiral staircase, we've managed to deliver excellent views over the Diglis Basin."

It's this focus on designing for the individual and a real passion for problem-solving that resonates so strongly with their clients. "Take The Regal Cinema in Evesham, for example. The big challenge here was to ensure the beautiful 1930s Art Deco building was brought up to current building standards without interfering with the aesthetics. This meant not visibly scattering the ceiling with fire alarm detectors or plastering the doors with 'keep shut' signs to meet the needs of fire regulations," Victoria recounts. "The elements are all there, they're just not screaming out at you." Poole Phillips' work at The Regal won local and regional awards, as did its conservation and sustainability work at Hill Top Farm in Grafton Flyford.

And all this is happening from Pershore's High Street. Victoria highlights, "We chose Pershore because it has everything to hand, it's compact, well-connected and we can reach our London-based clients in just two hours by train. Our team love where we are as well. They're always using the leisure centre for a good workout, whereas you're more likely to find me walking my dog by the river!"

44.

Derrick Barker

JMDA

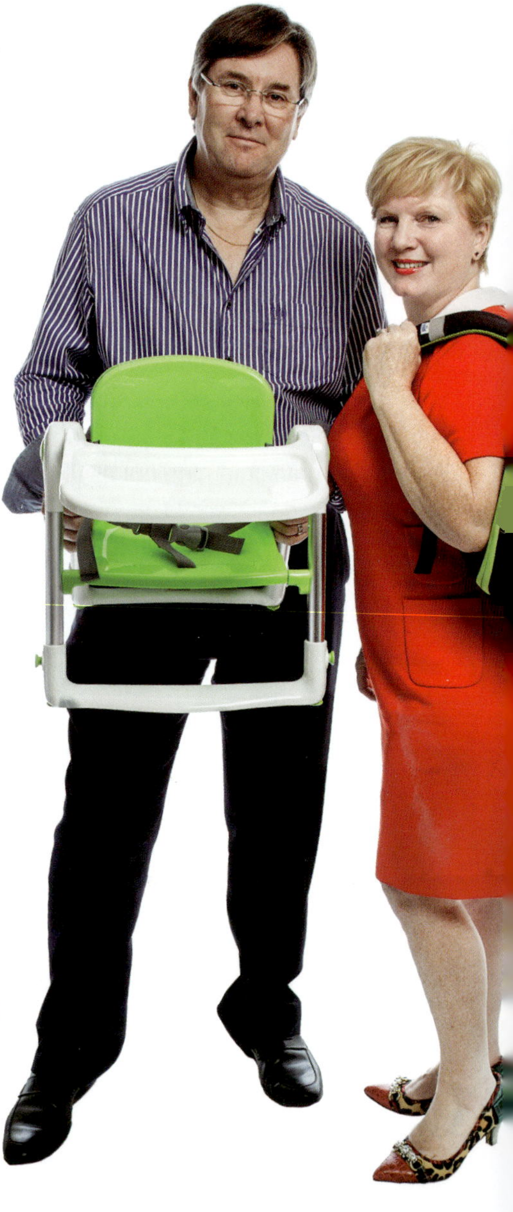

Product design and consultants

Business start date
2001

Number of employees
8

Location
Hill Furze, near Evesham

www.jmdadesign.com

Derrick's business lesson

"It's often said that every product has its moment when the time is right. I developed the idea of our first booster seat years ago and it didn't go anywhere until legislation changed, so don't give up."

Derrick Barker is always looking for innovative new ways to improve everyday products. One thing that doesn't need improving though, is the location of his office.

"A beautiful view definitely helps to get the creative juices flowing," smiles Derrick Barker. And when you're the Managing Director of a product design company, that creativity is vital. "We act as a think tank for our clients," he explains. "They come to us with an idea and we expand and improve on it, using our knowledge, expertise and creativity."

Back in 1991, Derrick and Cherril Barker started JMDA Product Design Consultancy servicing UK industry. It wasn't long before Derrick identified a need for a unique car seat for their children. A product idea was born.

JMDA's first major success came in the form of the Trunki BoostApack, which was a booster seat that doubled up as a rucksack. Derrick says, "A few years ago, legal requirements changed and it became compulsory for all children under the age of 12 to have a booster seat. Together with a company called Magmatic, we developed a product that was hand-luggage size and easy to transport. We sold the rights to Magmatic, and that's really when we took off developing our own products."

Since then more unique products have been developed extensively by Derrick and his team. From the Sit and See stadium booster seat, which allows children to get a better view at sporting events, to the car booster seat with in-built lights that means children can read and play in the dark, and most recently, the flat fold dining booster seat. The business specialises in children's products and Derrick's recognised as being a leading expert in car seat design.

But JMDA don't just focus on children's products. They work across a wide variety of different sectors, from the security industry to first aid products. They're also prominent in the bathroom fittings sector, having developed everything from shower cubicles to taps. As Derrick explains, "Our broad cross-section of products really helps to separate us from our competitors. We're also a global brand, as we have offices in Shanghai. It's a growing market and we get a lot of interest from international customers so it made sense to open up an office over there."

From the bright lights of Shanghai to the rural quietness of Worcestershire, Derrick and Cherril wouldn't ever consider moving the main offices out of Wychavon. Not only do they praise the rural setting for being a great backdrop for inspiration, but it's a big talking point for their customers too. "We have a video that we show to clients and it opens with a big heart that's beating in the centre of England. We're proud to be based here," he says. "A lot of the people we work with in China and America think England is like London and they're always pleasantly surprised when they come and see us in the countryside. Even our UK-based customers comment on it! They marvel at the fact there's no rushing traffic outside the office, and at the beauty of our barn-conversion offices."

45.

Kim Beckley

Kim Jewellery Ltd

Independent jewellery maker and designer selling one of a kind and limited edition jewellery in silver, gold and platinum

Business start date
2007

Number of employees
1

Location
Riverside Centre, Evesham

www.kimjewellery.co.uk

Kim's business lesson

"If you've got a dream, just go for it. You'll learn from your mistakes so stay positive."

Kim Beckley gets to spend her days sitting in a life-sized jewellery box, surrounded by sparkly gems and precious metals.

One thing that always surprises jewellery maker Kim is how many men come into her shop on Christmas Eve. "We get so many husbands and boyfriends coming in at about 2pm. They're all in a desperate panic, looking for something special to give to their partner and they end up just picking anything," she exclaims. "But jewellery is such a personal thing and people have very specific tastes. My advice is to have a look at what your loved ones have already, or take a walk by the shop and see if anything takes their fancy. Then come back another time to buy!"

Kim has a real passion for great design and craftsmanship and this is reflected in her collections from a range of national and international designers. But talk of designers shouldn't make you think that Kim's shop is pretentious, as she goes out of her way to welcome customers.

Kim explains, "The atmosphere is very relaxed and we provide a friendly service to all our customers. Alongside the range of designer pieces, I also make a lot of the jewellery myself. I sell a wide range of gift items in silver, gold with stones and without, and to suit a range of budgets."

Kim's been working with jewellery all her life and she specialises in hand-crafted pieces that she's designed herself. But she also offers a range of other services, including repair work and re-crafting. "There's a growing trend amongst divorcees to turn their wedding rings into new pieces of jewellery and I've been doing more and more of these recently."

Kim comments. "I also get asked quite frequently to seal the ashes of loved ones into pendants or put them into rings so they can wear them. It's quite a strange feeling, having someone's ashes on my workbench, but I never turn down these kind of jobs because I know how much they mean to people."

Born in South Korea but raised in Barbados before moving to Europe when she was 15, Kim has lived all over the world. But it's the beautiful countryside around Evesham that brought her back to the UK seven years ago. She comments, "I love the Cotswolds and the Evesham area, I love the river, the Malvern Hills, the architecture and the parks. Evesham has a lovely feel to it and I just fell in love with the town. Plus, my mum lives just around the corner and she's a great babysitter!" It's not just the scenic views that Kim loves though, having everything so close is handy for the busy working mum

46.

Rod Smith

Winstanley & Co

Specialist metal fabricators

Business start date
1877

Number of employees
80

Location
Pershore

www.winstanleyco.co.uk

Rod's business lesson

"Make sure you've done your research thoroughly and you know your industry inside out."

Winstanley specialist metal fabricators have been manufacturing components from sheet metal for over 130 years. But what is it that keeps them in Pershore?

As a world-class market leader, it's no surprise that fabrication specialists Winstanley work across a range of sectors, from the defence industry to the rail sector and plenty in between. No two days are ever the same.

One day, they're manufacturing non-lethal military equipment, the next, it's rail car interiors. Rod Smith, Managing Director at Winstanley, explains, "We manufacture components from sheet metal, and this can vary from big structures such as oil and gas frames to small components for agricultural vehicles. Having a diverse range of clients mean that if a sector goes through a quiet spell, it's not going to have a big impact on us as a business. Plus, it gives us a good edge over our competitors because we're experienced in different areas."

Established in 1877, the business has been around for a long time. And it's this longevity that evokes confidence in Winstanley's existing and potential clients. Rod says, "We're really proud of our history. Nowadays, there's nervousness about faceless businesses that are here today and gone the next. But we've been around for over 130 years and continue to offer the same great services and products that we've always done."

And Winstanley aren't planning on going anywhere just yet. "As a whole, the manufacturing industry is doing well at the moment, and we're just as strong as ever," he comments. "The fact that we supply a lot of overseas companies, who have bought British companies, proves that we can manufacture with the best of them. These big companies place their faith in us to deliver, and we always do."

For Rod, the most exciting thing about the future of the business is the potential of the people who work at the company. "We've got some fantastic apprentices with us at the moment and it's great to see them developing and being promoted," he says. "The best bit is that the majority of them are from the Wychavon area. I strongly believe there's a lot of untapped potential around here and it's rewarding to be able to say that we've helped to lay the foundations for the fabricators of tomorrow.

"We're recruiting apprentices who are mainly doing welding or engineering courses, and are thrilled to be given the chance to work and learn at Winstanley. Our Co-Director was 17 when he started here, sweeping the floor. Now he owns 20 percent of the company. That's the kind of person we're looking for, and we're confident that we're in the best place to find them. That's why we're not looking to move anywhere else!"

47.

Chris Ward

Farncombe Estate

Hospitality on a private 400-acre country estate in the Cotswolds

Business start date
Hotel - 1978
Conference Venue - 2001

Number of employees
150

Location
Broadway

www.farncombeestate.co.uk

Chris's business lesson

"Never lose sight of your long-term vision. Keep your eye on what you're trying to achieve in the future, otherwise you'll never get there."

With breathtaking views across the Cotswolds it's been described as a cross between Provence and the Italian lakes, but there's so much more to Farncombe Estate than just a beautiful location.

Set on 400 acres of rolling countryside and with unspoilt views across Broadway and Evesham, the privately owned Farncombe Estate is the embodiment of dramatic luxury. It is best described as an exclusive range of hospitality and leisure businesses.

In a previous life, Farncombe Estate was used as the private headquarters of a security firm and it's only in the last decade that the grounds have been opened up. Chris Ward, Commercial Director at Farncombe Estate explains, "There's an old saying about the grounds that the security barriers used to be firmly down around the estate. But now the security firm has moved and the estate is widely accessible, our challenge is to give people a reason to come and visit us."

And give them a reason they have. One of the most impressive buildings on the estate is the Dormy House Hotel. The family-run hotel has recently undergone a huge renovation project to turn it into a beautiful hotel that's the epitome of 'farmhouse chic'. Chris comments, "The house has been around since the 17th century and it's a beautiful building. We wanted to give it a new lease of life, which is how the project came about. It's incredibly sumptuous, and it's a real Cotswold home. It's modern and stylish but there's still the old exposed Cotswold stone. It's a great mix of old and new and we like to encourage our guests to think of it as a home, but better."

Chris and the team are also in the middle of developing a sparkling new health spa that's set to open at Dormy House in 2014. Spread across three floors, the beauty spa has a (Veuve Clicquot-sponsored) champagne nail bar, an infinity swimming pool, a gym and a separate personal training studio.

Farncombe Estate certainly understands its customers "Offering visitors a relaxed kind of luxury is what we aim for," Explains Chris. "There's certainly an appetite among consumers today for quality. There are lots of great hotels in the area but there aren't many that offer what we do, and we don't charge the earth for it either. We're able to offer a great experience along with a range of leisure activities, including golf. We're neighboured by Broadway Golf Club and our guests are able to use their facilities, which is an added bonus."

The estate doesn't just appeal to those looking to get away for the weekend. There are also two restaurants within the hotel that are popular among the locals. The Potting Shed offers pub style food in a relaxed setting, while The Garden Room offers a somewhat fancier experience that's open for dinner and Sunday lunches. Being able to recognise the different types of customers has been key in the success of these restaurants. Chris explains, "We know that the people who come in to eat with us are different from those who are staying with us so we have to adapt our message. They want a different experience so it's important to make sure we offer what they're after."

Elsewhere on the estate, there's also Farncombe Conference Centre. The 89-bedroom conference village is ideal for meetings, conferences, training and team building. In fact they offer one of the widest selections of team-building activities in the UK, ranging from treasure hunts to problem solving and communication tasks. At weekends, the conference centre is home to Farncombe Courses. Offering a wide range of leisure courses for adults including residential weekend study breaks and day courses, it's popular with special interest groups, who come to learn and study in the peaceful surroundings. Recent residents include yoga groups, singers and guitarists.

Chris relishes the challenge of appealing to his diverse customer base. "People love the area and travel here to see it. But we don't rely on the area to bring us business and we're always looking at different ways to develop. The future's going to be bright for Farncombe Estate."

48.

Brian Barber

British Horticultural Growers Sundries Ltd

One stop shop for all professional and amateur horticultural and florist supplies

Business start date
1908

Number of employees
47

Location
Vale Park, Evesham

www.bhgsltd.co.uk

Brian's business lesson

"Treat people as you'd like to be treated. You'll leave a great impression behind."

If you're serious about gardening, take a trip to British Horticultural Growers Sundries Ltd (BHGS). The Evesham-based business is a favourite among professional and amateur growers throughout the Vale and beyond. It also caters for large estates and allotment societies.

When Littleton and Badsey Growers Ltd was set up in 1908 by the founding Chairman Charles Binyon, in the picture held by Brian, it was set up as a co-operative with just a few interested growers. Who could have thought that after one hundred years, although no longer a co-operative, the ethos would remain the same? And with 450 shareholders and over 2,000 account customers the business continues to grow and grow.

Brian Barber, General Manager at BHGS says, "When Charles Binyon founded this business it was set up to bring together local growers and strengthen marketing and purchasing power. Everyone involved in the business was an investor and everyone worked hard to make the business succeed. We're a limited company now but there is still that same kind of 'family' feel to BHGS and several employees have become shareholders. We always maintain that horticulture is a 'people business' and our colleagues are really important to us. We take the pastoral care of them really seriously. Several of them have been with us for over thirty years."

Based in the very fertile Vale of Evesham, BHGS provide a one stop shop for peat, compost, fertilisers, chemicals, pots, canes and much more. They deliver within a radius of 120 miles of Evesham to professional growers of salad crops, vegetables, bedding plant producers, nursery stock growers, allotment societies and large estates. Fulfilling a genuine need in the area for people who are serious about gardening and growing. BHGS are able to provide expert knowledge and advice about all things horticultural. "Serious amateurs can get products from us that they may find difficult to get elsewhere," says Brian.

With a history spanning over 100 years, diversifying has been key to the success. Brian says, "It's so important to adapt to what is going on around you. Thirty years ago we were solely catering for the glass-house industry, outdoor vegetable and fruit growers. Over the years, this has changed in favour of nursery stock and bedding and pot plant production."

BHGS has also become known for the largest selection of artificial flowers within the area and employs a qualified florist to merchandise and provide expert advice. What started out as something to increase business during the quiet months, between October and January, has now become a business in its own right.

"Our floral art business has proven very popular," enthuses Brian. "Initially we dipped our toe in the water with wreath frames and plastic flowers. Over the years we have increased our stock and supply high quality flowers and florist supplies. We have opened a wedding hire section and also provide a wedding flower service by way of marquee decoration and bridal bouquets. We can honestly say we provide 'bouquets for life!'"

For Brian, the most exciting aspect of being involved in a company like BHGS is the unknown. He smiles, "The British climate makes it interesting. No month is ever the same and we have to make sure we're on top of our game to react to whatever it throws at us." With a wry smile he adds, "I've also met some wonderful characters along the way."

49.

Judith Synnuck

The Little Shoe Box

Specialist shoe fitting

Business start date
2004

Number of employees
2

Location
The Royal Arcade, Pershore

www.widerfitshoes.co.uk

Judith's business lesson

"It's never too late to learn, and the more people you speak to, the more you learn."

It's a case of "Saturday job turned day job" for Judith Synnuck, who runs The Little Shoe Box, a specialist shoe fitting centre in Pershore.

The prospect of redundancy after 23 years spent building a career would be a big concern for anyone, but for Judith it also meant a loss of identity. Thinking about where to focus her attention, and knowing that she wanted a different challenge, Judith heard that Pershore was in desperate need for someone to open up a shoe stall - after the previous, well-established business had closed two years earlier. Shoes evoked happy memories for Judith, all her Saturdays during college had been spent in shoe shops, measuring children's feet in Clarks or working in the Russell & Bromley shoe shop in Worcester, when it first opened.

Judith explains, "My sister-in-law had a stall on Pershore market at the time and when she mentioned the gap in the market for a shoe seller, I definitely had an 'I can do that!' moment." Knowing that Pershore had an older demographic and that having the right type of product would be the difference between success and failure, I managed to speak to the previous stall holder and she kindly put me in touch with a couple of local warehouses. Her advice was invaluable." In addition to attending a business set-up course, Judith was given a grant by Wychavon District Council, which she put towards fixtures and fittings and promoting her niche offering.

The Little Shoe Box stall opened in March 2004, and soon Judith was opening up additional units to meet the growing demands of her customers. It wasn't long before the market stall was swapped for retail premises in The Royal Arcade, where Judith still trades now.

"I really got to know my customers well and understood that well-fitting high-quality shoes were really important to them," Judith comments. "Some of my customers have bespoke needs and I am now one of just four specialist fitting centres in the UK, selling shoes from the British brand DB that offers shoes in an extra-wide fit. I have regular customers who travel over the Welsh border to see me. They park easily and for free outside my shop, come in for an hour's appointment, and then go off and enjoy a lovely day out in Pershore. They make a day of it!"

The community spirit in Pershore has really made a difference for Judith. Just as she opened her shop she sadly lost her husband and Judith says that the support she received from the business community and customers was fantastic. "They were like an extended family to me," she explains. "They encouraged me to get involved in local events such as Pershore's Plum Festival and to get out and network. In my opinion, it's never too late to learn and the more people you speak to, the more you learn."

Judith describes Pershore as "an old-fashioned town with a future". She says, "In a world where personal service is often lacking, the little things like remembering where a customer went on holiday or asking about a recent family birthday means a great deal to people. It makes them feel special."

50.

John Jenkinson

The Evesham Hotel

Hotel and restaurant

Business start date
1975

Number of employees
40-50

Location
Evesham

www.eveshamhotel.com

John's business lesson

"Stick to your principles. Cutting corners might seem like a good idea in the short - term, but customers will remain loyal if they know they'll always get a good service, so make sure not to compromise in the long-term."

The Evesham Hotel is a quirky little treasure nestled in the Vale of Evesham and it's got quite a reputation.

Owners John and Sue Jenkinson have a simple motto when it comes to business, "Always make sure you're having fun! If you're enjoying what you're doing then your customers will enjoy it and they'll keep coming back." And they're certainly taking heed of their own advice. The hotel is famous for being eccentric, with a telephone box standing proudly next to the indoor swimming pool, a talking mirror in the ladies toilets and lots of signs and interesting collectables to keep visitors occupied for hours. And every visitor gets a room key with a teddy attached!

John and Sue have owned the hotel since 1975, and together have worked hard to grow and develop the business. John explains, "When we were handed the keys all those years ago, it was a small hotel with 18 bedrooms and very little passing trade. We've since built it up to have 40 rooms and an indoor swimming pool and we've always got guests staying with us." Now, the hotel has won a host of awards, including being listed in 1998 as one of the best ten hotels in the British Isles by the founding editor of the Good Hotel Guide. They've even won awards for their unique toilets!

It's not just the hotel that gets glowing reviews from visitors. The adjoining restaurant is famed for the delicious breakfasts and the variety of meals on offer for lunch and dinner. "We try to be as accommodating as possible for our guests and when we have overseas visitors and they start to get a little bit homesick, our chef is always happy to cook them up a little something to remind them of home. We've even had a guest come into the kitchen before to show us how it's done."

John and Sue are keen to support local businesses and a lot of the ingredients used in the kitchen are locally sourced, but the central location means that even ingredients from a little further away can still be delivered fresh to them. John comments, "Our fish, is more often than not, delivered on the same afternoon that it was caught. Because we're so central, it only takes a couple of hours to get here. Most of it comes from Cornwall but we have suppliers all around the coast."

The location has also helped the hotel to become what it is today. John and Sue love the hotel's quirky reputation, but believe that if the hotel had been based anywhere else, it wouldn't have worked. I think we would have had to take it down a different route, which wouldn't have been so much fun," John says. "All of our employees are local too, and they're an incredibly important part of the business. Without them, the hotel just wouldn't have the same feel to it."

John's eccentricity extends to his transport habits too. He's often spotted driving around Evesham in his trusty old Sinclair C5, branded up with the hotel's logo of course!

TELEPHONE

51.

Roger Dyson

Roger Dyson Ltd and Hardings Travel

Breakdown truck manufacturer and premier coach tour operator

Business start date
1969

Number of employees
85+

Location
Berry Hill Trading Estate, Droitwich Spa

www.rogerdyson.com

Roger's business lesson

"Be determined and don't give up. Don't rush things, take a long-term view, be patient and put in the effort, it's worth it in the end."

Roger Dyson always wanted to run his own business. He didn't enjoy school and left at 15 to work full time in garages. It was a motorbike accident that enabled Roger to set up his repair business and find his niche doing vehicle recovery.

Roger explains, "I was involved in a motorbike accident when I was 17, which wasn't my fault. I received £300 compensation, which seemed a fortune at that time and used it to start my motor repair business doing all sorts of repairs on cars and commercial vehicles. I soon realised I needed to tow vehicles in, so I built a machine from second-hand parts for vehicle recovery."

It wasn't long before Roger designed and developed his first professionally built recovery unit from new parts. He'd spotted a gap in the market and there was a huge demand for his recovery vehicles.

Today, Roger Dyson Ltd is the UK's largest manufacturer of vehicle recovery equipment, manufacturing three new recovery vehicles a week, with sales over £9 million per year, employing over 85 people. This includes Roger's other business Hardings Travel of Worcestershire – a coach tour operator that he runs with his brother on his 3.5 acre site on Berry Hill Trading Estate in Droitwich Spa.

The business now supplies breakdown trucks to clients including RAC, AA, police forces, local councils and even the Channel Tunnel. They even export to countries around the world, including South Africa and Australia.

Roger explains, "People want to buy British, as we have a reputation for quality, and being based in Droitwich Spa is perfect for us as we're located between junctions 5 and 6 of the M5. We're easy to get to."

Roger believes his success is due to the commitment and work ethic of his team," He says. "We employ local people who stay with us, some employees have been here over twenty years. We give our people a pre-Christmas bonus, everyone gets the same amount regardless of salary and it helps keep people motivated. We're interested in our people but we know they have a life outside of work."

The two businesses work well together. "We share human resources, finance and marketing skills across both companies," Roger comments.

It's not always been easy for Roger and his business though. The recession was a real shock and forced him to have a good look at the business and how things are done. "It meant less work, we had to lay some people off and it forced us to take a real hard look at our costs. We thought we were efficient but the recession made us look critically at how we do things. We learnt a lot, and it taught us to tighten up and make improvements. We do take a cautious approach now to expansion because of the recession."

And expanding they are. In Roger's fortieth year in business he's looking for 20 new people and wants to carry on growing his businesses, but gradually and doing things properly. "We could double the coaching business as the demand for trips and holidays is really growing. But we want to get it right, we don't want to expand too rapidly," he concludes.

52.

Steve Davies

Media52

Website solutions and marketing agency

Business start date
2005

Number of employees
20

Location
Bishampton

www.media52.com

Steve's business lesson

"Identify what is hype and what is reality."

Steve Davies experienced and subsequently got fed up with packed trains, busy airports and the daily grind of the commuter rat race. He longed for a more peaceful creative environment for his web and marketing business.

And lucky for Steve he found it in an idyllic converted barn on the outskirts of Bishampton. It was the right decision for Steve as he explains, "With only tractors as traffic and fields filled with cows as a view, I knew it was the perfect choice for Media52. Our client base is as much international as it is local, so I had the luxury of selecting a location without any real restrictions."

But the decision hasn't just been to the benefit of the staff and Steve. Clients and suppliers all remark on what a pleasure it is to get out of the city, away from the stress and noise to meet in the picturesque countryside.

Steve continues, "Given the rural nature of Wychavon, it's surprisingly convenient. Whether you're travelling from the north, south, east or west, you're only 20 minutes from the motorway network or the nearest mainline station."

Steve truly believes that the location of the business gives them a competitive edge. "In today's evolving digital landscape, the calming nature of our studio is conducive to our technical, creative and marketing tasks. We're a close knit group of people who enjoy our working environment. The tranquillity of our surroundings aids our creative thought process."

The future is bright for Media52 with some rapidly expanding international markets meaning global satellite offices will need to be established to keep up with the demand. The agency also has a strong focus on new technologies and is always on the look out for the next big thing and more importantly, getting there first.